May 2, 1996

To Jim & Lois,
May you
are well and in
good health.
All my best,
Rachelle Doorman

D1301057

AGING INTO THE 21st CENTURY

The Exploration of Aspirations and Values

AGING INTO THE 21st CENTURY

The Exploration of Aspirations and Values

RACHELLE A. DORFMAN, Ph.D.
School of Social Welfare
University of California, Los Angeles

BRUNNER/MAZEL *Publishers* • NEW YORK

Library of Congress Cataloging-in-Publication Data

Dorfman, Rachelle A.
    Aging into the 21st century : the exploration of aspirations and values
Rachelle A. Dorfman.
        p.   cm.
    Includes bibliographical references and indexes.
    ISBN 0-87630-643-1
    1. Aged—Psychology.   2. Aged—Health and hygiene.   I. Title.
    [DNLM: 1. Aged—psychology.   2. Aspirations (Psychology)—in old
age.   3. Social Values—in old age.   WT 150 D695i 1993]
BF724.8.D67   1993
155.67—dc20
DNLM/DLC
for Library of Congress

                                                        93-11673
                                                        CIP

Copyright © 1994 by Brunner/Mazel, Inc.

All rights reserved. No part of this book may be
reproduced by any process whatsoever without
the written permission of the copyright owner.

Published by
BRUNNER/MAZEL, INC.
19 Union Square West
New York, New York 10003

Manufactured in the United States of America

10   9   8   7   6   5   4   3   2   1

This book is dedicated to the memory of
Ruth Kress
who gave her love unconditionally
and to
Rose Fishman
who inspired us with her spirit

CONTENTS

FOREWORD

It is surprising how much has been written about aging from the outside. Here is a book that takes an inside view of aging. Older people are portrayed as thinking, feeling, and decision-making adults, not as a statistical "they." Here we have a book that takes us into the insides of aging where individual values and aspirations come alive in a very personal sense. Rachelle Dorfman begins with her experiences in obtaining older people's inner views about life and then walks us back to the outer view where they become an object.

In the scientific study of aging, older persons are usually viewed as objects with little recognition of their awareness or self-determination. This inside view of aging indicates that older persons are still directing their own efforts at transcending the limitations in their lives that have accompanied old age.

We all have to confront reality and the reality for the readers of this book is a balance of what the inside view of old age reveals and what the external views of social scientists and professionals tell us about life and circumstances of the aged. The individuals we get acquainted with in this book are trying to live out their later years according to their values. This is best done in a "value friendly" long-term care atmosphere. Rachelle Dorfman presents us with a blend of both the inside and outside views of aging in enough detail that we get a close up picture of what it means to be old in an American institutional setting. It is said you can't smell the roses from your automobile while driving on a freeway. The book walks us through lives at a pace so that we can see and smell the rose of old age. Those interested in the quality of life in institutions for the aged will find this book a revealing guide.

JAMES E. BIRREN, PH.D.

ACKNOWLEDGMENTS

The writing of this book and the research that preceded it were motivated by my desire to understand the aging experience. This endeavor required considerable effort on my part. It also required the involvement, support, and encouragement of dozens of colleagues, family members, and friends.

First—and most important—I want to thank the residents of "Franklin Village"* who so graciously opened up their hearts and minds (as well as their homes) to me. Their wisdom and kindness has enhanced my life and given me a deeper understanding of the aging process, with all of its joys and challenges.

I am indebted to Hugh Rosen, who will always be my intellectual inspiration, and to Jerome Allender, Jennie Keith, and Curt Torell, who stood up for me when others doubted that my research could or should be done. Elsa Efran has my gratitude and admiration for her editorial skills.

Every author needs a person who identifies problems and resolves them with great calm and intelligence. I found these qualities in my research assistants, Connie Wynne and Phil Meyer. I thank Connie and Phil and all of the students and colleagues who provided feedback and suggestions on the manuscript.

Early on, the School of Health Sciences and Humanities and the Department of Mental Health Sciences of Hahnemann Uni-

---

*To protect the privacy of the community and its residents, all names and certain identifying characteristics have been changed.

versity in Philadelphia generously supported the hours I spent in the field. Later on, Dean Rosina Becerra and Associate Dean James Lubben at The School of Social Welfare, University of California, Los Angeles, provided additional support and encouragement as I spent even more hours struggling to communicate what I had learned.

I am especially grateful to my loving parents, Frances and Frank Abramson, and my children, Holly, Howard, Jeff, and Sarri.

The pleasure of producing this work is exceeded by only one other production—the little guy who has made me a grandmother. I love you, Shawn Michael Kaplan.

R.A.D.

INTRODUCTION

The media, the politicians, and the health care professionals have done their jobs. Nearly everyone in America is aware that our population is aging rapidly. It is especially striking when one considers that between 1960 and 1990, the number of people over age 85 increased by 232%, while the rest of the population increased by only 39%.*

This is only the beginning. The Census Bureau estimates that there will be about 12 million people over age 85 in 2040.† Other sources have doubled or even tripled that estimate. Thus, the likelihood of living to a "ripe old age" is more of a reality now than ever before. Herein lies the motivation for writing this book. We know little about the experience of old age, and even less about how to ensure a happy and meaningful existence well into the seventh, eighth, or even ninth decade of life.

This book represents my personal odyssey into the inner experience of aging. The journey begins with my immersion into a community of elders and the honing of my observational skills. It ends with a clearer understanding of the phenomenology of aging—one that is divested of ageist myths and stereotypes and that highlights the significance of aspirations and values in late life.

This volume could be categorized as a book on *gerontology*— the study of the biological, psychological, and social aspects of

---

Profiles of America's Elderly: Growth of America's Elderly in the 1980s (No. 2, July 1992). Washington, DC: U.S. Bureau of the Census and the National Institute on Aging.
†Ibid.

aging—although admittedly it is light on the biological aspects. More accurately, it is a book about *social gerontology*, which is the study of the ways in which aging and the aged affect the development of social institutions and policies and the ways in which social and cultural conditions affect the lives of the elderly.

We can place this text under still more rubrics. For example, it is also a book about ethnography—a method that is particularly well-suited for gerontological research. In ethnographic studies, researchers become members of the communities they study. They observe and record descriptions of the behaviors and the thoughts and feelings that will eventually illuminate the subjective experience of their informants. The researcher's task is not only to communicate an accurate representation of that which is studied but also to proceed to concept development and theory building. Furthermore, it is a "how to" book, replete with applications for long-term care and psychotherapy for older adults.

The setting, Franklin Village, is a continuing care retirement community. In my view, it is a nearly ideal environment in which to live out one's last years. Residents have what all of us would like for those we love—safety; security; companionship; accessible high-quality health care; comfortable, attractive homes with nutritious, tasty meals; and the freedom and support to pursue whatever stimulation, pastime, or degree of independence they desire. There is, for all who dwell there, great comfort in knowing that to the end of their days, despite frailty or dementia, their needs will continue to be met with skill and kindness, and without threat of increased financial burden to themselves or their families.

In Part I (Chapters 1 and 2), I attempt to give the reader a sense of what it is like to be old in America, with its history of age discrimination and negative stereotyping. I lay out my research plans, struggle to gain entry into Franklin Village, and begin to develop relationships with men and women, whom I initially conceive of as subjects, but soon embrace as friends.

Part II (Chapters 3 through 7) is organized by the underlying values (autonomy, personal growth, helping, social ties, and pleasure) that drive the hopes and dreams of Franklin Village residents. Each value, expressed in the voices of the residents, becomes the data with which I must grapple.

In Part III (Chapters 8 through 10), I explore the genesis of values, value systems, and value dilemmas in old age, which helped me understand the residents' aspirations and the sense of well-being I observed in the community. Finally, I consider the implications of what I have learned for the development of long-term care environments and the practice of psychotherapy.

This book is written for the student and the professional, but also for those who are (or will be) affected by an aging society. In other words, this book will be useful for anyone who delivers services to elders, creates programs, develops policies—or *who is growing older.*

Because I wished to make such a work "user-friendly," I created a glossary. Most of the italicized words in the text can be found there. I also created three resource guides. One lists professional organizations, another comprises groups that will be of value to either professionals or consumers, and a third lists only those designed for consumers' needs. I have found that most "aging directories" are woefully inaccurate. I suspect that many of the errors in these publications are perpetuated because the information was merely copied from other faulty or out-of-date directories. The information in these resource directories, however, was meticulously checked at the time of writing and once again just before the presses rolled. If there are errors, no doubt it is because organizations and agencies have since relocated, merged, or shut their doors.

Finally, I must once again thank my friends at Franklin Village. Of all the wonderful lessons you taught me, the most important is, as Robert Browning said, "the best is yet to be."*

R.A.D.

---

*"Rabbi Ben Ezra," in John Pettigrew (Ed.). (1981). *Robert Browning: The poems* (Vol. 1, p. 781). New York: Penguin Books.

PART I

THE LATER YEARS

CHAPTER 1

THE EXPERIENCE OF AGING

In the mountains of Ohai, California, potter Mary Stoner* toils at her craft for 12 hours each day. She is 97 years old. In Hamburg, Pennsylvania, Charlie Shore and eight members of his "Geritol Gang" gather at the base of Blue Mountain for their daily hike on the Appalachian Trail. The gang members, ranging in age from 67 to 75, will trim the brush, mark the trail, and repair anything that is out of place. Thousands of miles away, in Quezaltenango, Guatemala, Joan Mayfield, a Peace Corps volunteer, supervises a weaving cooperative of 400 women. Joan is 77 years old.

Meanwhile, in the Fairfax district of Los Angeles, diminutive 68-year-old Selma Gold passes the day by watching television. Eleven plastic containers from the neighborhood pharmacy are lined up in a neat row on a nearby table. One is for her arthritis, two are for her hypertension, one is to settle her nervous stomach, and one is to help her sleep. There are eye drops for her glaucoma, pills to counteract the side effects of other pills, and several bottles whose purposes are unclear. When a visiting social worker asks, "What do you do all day?" Selma replies, "I take medicine."

In an old, run-down home, not far away from Selma's neighborhood, lives 77-year-old George Miller. According to his doctor, George is in good health and should be enjoying the economic security of a good pension and careful retirement planning. However, he rarely leaves the house. After his wife died

---

*All names have been changed to protect privacy.

three years ago, George began to use alcohol to help him face loneliness and despair. Relatives are startled by George's appearance and obvious decline. He is not unaware of the changes, but he attributes them to being "an old man."

These examples of old age are familiar. In recent years, the public's consciousness about aging has been raised. We read about 75-year-old marathon runners and weight-lifters, and we view documentaries about the plight of Alzheimer's patients and their families. We read about grandmothers who are raising "crack" babies with extraordinary sensitivity and compassion, and we are aware of other grandmothers whose needs for care are equal to those of the crack babies.

These extreme examples of aging in American society distort our view of what is "normal." Average men and women have no conception of what to expect when they become old. The optimistic among them point to alert, active octogenarians and envision the same type of old age for themselves. More common, however, are those who regard the later years (when they allow themselves to think about it) with dread, fearing dependency, poor health, mental decline, and economic disaster.

Unfortunately, some of these fears are well-founded. We live in an ageist society, which means that some elderly have difficulty obtaining adequate housing, health care, employment, and the satisfactions of positive regard from others and from themselves. Physical changes brought about by the aging process, as well as chronic diseases and conditions associated with increasing age, contribute to older people's actual or imagined frailty and their vulnerability to financial indigence, victimization, social isolation, and mental-health problems.

Research on aging generally focuses on diminishments in biological functioning (e.g., kidney function, cardiac output), changes in the capacity for self-regulation (e.g., decreased ability to regulate body temperature and blood pressure), and changes in appearance (e.g., graying hair, redistribution of fat, and loss of muscle mass). Research in the psychological domain investigates losses in sensory acuity, cognition (e.g., memory and learning), and emotion (e.g., pathological bereavement and mental illness). Studies in the sociological sphere emphasize role loss, loss of social status, and social withdrawal.

These aspects of aging are relatively simple to define and measure. Changes are easily *quantified* and lend themselves to sophisticated *statistical analysis*. Although such research findings further our understanding of normal aging, they reveal only part of the story—which could be graphically represented as a downward curve.

The aspects of aging that do not lend themselves to precise measurement include wisdom, spiritual harmony, compassion, acceptance, and insight. These are the "fruits of old age," but they receive little press. They are, at best, ill-defined, and—from the vantage point of relative youth—they are merely weak consolation prizes for living a long time. These features could be represented by an upward curve.

The concept of dual curves is not new. Buhler (1935) first formulated this concept in the 1920s. She noted that the psychological curve (which represents productivity at work, the self, and life satisfaction) lags behind the biological curve (which represents bodily functions). She stated that although both domains ascend and descend, the psychological curve rises later, peaks later, and descends later than the biological curve.

This book explores the "upward curve"—the domain of inner experience. It attempts to illuminate the "human face of gerontology" (Moody, 1989), modify the pervasive negative view of what it means to be old, and advance the perception that *qualitative research methodology* is the approach of choice to achieve these goals.

AGEISM

An 87-year-old friend and resident of a nursing home recently said to me, "I think that God is punishing me by allowing me to live so long." She is in good health. Family members visit her regularly. The nursing home is clean and staffed with competent, kind people who are interested in her well-being. Yet life holds no joy for her. When asked to elaborate, she would only say, "Nobody likes old people." In that simple phrase, she embodied all the negative stereotyping and discrimination directed against people who are old.

Robert Butler, who was director of the National Institute on Aging from 1974 to 1982, coined the term *ageism* (Butler, 1969) to describe the "stereotypes and myths, outright disdain and dislike, or simply subtle avoidance of contact; discriminatory practices in housing, employment and services of all kinds; epithets, cartoons and jokes" (Butler, 1975, p. 12) suffered by old people in the United States. His Pulitzer-Prize-winning book, *Why Survive?*, starkly exposed the tragedy of growing old in America, and it popularized the notion of ageism.

Membership in the "correct" groups helps one to escape being victimized by "isms." However, ageism, unlike racism and sexism, cannot be escaped—unless one dies early. Some people have called ageism the ultimate prejudice, the last discrimination, and the cruelest rejection.

Dislike for older people has not always been the rule. Prior to the mid-1800s, many people believed that the soul developed gradually. This belief contributed to a widespread preference for age and to an age-related hierarchy in social and family relations (Cole, 1979). Prejudice and discrimination were usually directed against younger people because of their assumed immaturity and lack of wisdom (Palmore, 1990).

Examples of how this situation has changed can be found in U.S. census reports. In the 1776 and 1787 reports for Maryland and Connecticut, age biases ran counter to modern censuses. An excessive number of people claimed to be 41 or 51, showing a clear preference for greater age. In modern censuses, the opposite is true; excessive numbers of people claim to be 39 or 49 (Fischer, 1978, quoted in Gratton, 1985).

Two major viewpoints account for this change in age preference. The traditional *modernization theory* argues that *structural forces*, primarily industrialization and urbanization, dramatically changed the way older people were regarded. On the other side, proponents of *attitudinal forces* argue that the change was cultural—that is, changes in society's values were directly responsible for the devaluation of the elderly in a society that was increasingly placing youth and beauty above all else.

The ideas that were the basis of modernization theory were first espoused by supporters of old-age pensions. Epstein (1933), an early and persistent advocate for old-age security, wrote that old people could not keep up with machines; once their impairments set in, they had to be eliminated from the work force for the good of business. He called them "drags" upon production.

Modernization theory is based on the notion that when agricultural society gave way to an industrial society, old people (no longer landowners and patriarchs of farm families) lost their authority. Former "older" landowners found themselves working in factories alongside young workers, many of whom were immigrants willing to work for lower wages. In an era of "scientific management," in which speed and strength were highly valued on assembly lines, the older worker was labeled "inferior."

Opponents of modernization theory argue that the loss of status occurred prior to industrialization. They hold that the decline of the veneration and the beginning of the vilification of old age began between 1770 and 1820 and was the result of new ideas about age. Negative references to the elderly in literary works of that period indicate a shattering of esteem for age (Fischer, 1978). Here, for example, is a poem by Walt Whitman (1931, p. 278):

A HAND MIRROR

Hold it up sternly-see this it sends back, (who is it? is it you?)
Outside fair costume, within ashes and filth,
No more a flashing eye, no more a sonorous voice or springy step,
Now some slave's eye, voice, hands, step,
A drunkard's breath, unwholesome eater's face, venerealee's flesh,

Lungs rotting away piecemeal, stomach sour and cankerous,
Joints rheumatic, bowels clogged with abomination,
Blood circulating dark and poisonous streams,
Words babble, hearing and touch callous,
No brain, no heart left, no magnetism of sex;
Such from one look in this looking-glass ere you go hence,
Such a result so soon—and from such a beginning!

Negative depictions of aging also arose in medicine. Science began to document *averages* in physical capacities and functioning of older people. When such averages were compared with the averages of young people, the older age groups appeared depressingly deteriorated.*

Religion also played a role in the evolution of negative attitudes towards aging. Calvinists, for example, assumed that it was normal to suffer physical and mental deterioration in the advanced years. To them, it was humankind's punishment for the sins of Adam. Victorian values included control over one's body. Physical decay represented failure and sin. It was generally believed by the revivalists and health reformers between 1830 and 1870 that if people worked hard, had faith, and practiced self-discipline, they would retain their health and independence well into old age. Only the shiftless, faithless, and promiscuous, it was thought, would die early or suffer a miserable old age (Cole, 1983).

More recently, social critics link the degradation and devaluation of the aged with the rise of the American "narcissistic per-

---

*It is important to underscore the significance of research methodology in the study of the elderly. If one compares, for example, the average height of 25-year-olds in 1993 with the average height of 75-year-olds in 1993, one will find several inches of difference. It is incorrect to assume from this *cross-sectional study* that people "shrink" 5 or 6 inches between 25 and 75. No one could possibly feel good about the aging process if this were true. However, if we had been able to trace the height changes of the same group of people over 50 years, from age 25 to 75 (a *longitudinal study*), changes related to age (such as osteoporosis or spinal-cord compression) would be obvious, but not as dramatic as one would observe in a cross-sectional study. We also need to be aware of the *cohort effect*, the observation that people who are born about the same time share similar life experiences that may contribute to phenomena unlike those that appear in different cohort groups. For instance, a 75-year-old cohort experienced a different health and nutritional experience than a 25-year-old cohort. This should be a significant consideration when comparing any two age groups along any dimension.

sonality" (Lasch, 1978), which dreads age and believes that old people are useless. Age discrimination is manifested in two ways: *institutional ageism*, in which the policy of an institution or a social structure discriminates against older people and in *personal ageism*, in which individuals hold negative beliefs and attitudes about the elderly, resulting in discrimination (Palmore, 1990). Examples of both forms can be found most noticeably in the workplace, in housing, and in health care. As noted earlier, the term ageism was coined almost 25 years ago and was originally used to describe the intensely negative feelings that emerged in a bitter dispute about a housing project. The public housing agency of the District of Columbia proposed purchasing a highrise apartment building in northwest Washington to house the elderly poor. Butler (1969) was struck by the personal revulsion and distaste for the old that was reflected in the neighborhood residents' angry protests.

It is unclear to what degree that kind of hostility still exists. However, Lawton and Hoffman (1984) report four cases in which local groups were so incensed at proposed housing for the aged that they took legal action to bar it. They feared that housing for the elderly would usher in housing for other racial or ethnic groups, that stigmatizing services (health services, senior citizen centers, health vans, etc.) would proliferate, and that the neighborhood would see an increased presence of people with obvious mental or physical disabilities.

When age discrimination in the workplace was first addressed in America in the 1930s, it was primarily concerned with the nonhiring of workers. However, when the issue emerged again during debates on the Civil Rights Act of 1964, it focused on forced retirement practices for those 65 years and older. As a result of those debates, the Secretary of Labor conducted a study that documented the existence of ageism in employment (U.S. Department of Labor, 1965), and legislation was passed to deal with it—the Age Discrimination in Employment Act of 1967. The act was designed to protect workers from age 40 to 65. In 1978, an amendment extended the protection to age 70. In 1984, the upper age limit for government employees was eliminated. In 1986, the Act was again amended to eradicate any age ceiling. There are only four exceptions: tenured faculty 70 years old and older; executives entitled to at least $44,000 a year in retirement benefits; public officials and their staffs not subject to civil service laws; and firefighters and law-enforcement personnel. However, the exceptions for firefighters, law-enforcement officers, and tenured professors will expire on December 31, 1993. These employees will then be included in the general unlimited prohibition of age discrimination.

In recent years, despite such legislation, claims of age discrimination have been increasing at a rate proportionally higher than claims of race and sex discrimination (Eglit, 1989). Even more striking is the 1986 Gallup Poll that reported that 95% of those who believed they had experienced age discrimination had taken no action (cited in Lindeman, 1987).

Health care is a third area of discrimination that has been well-documented. Many elderly people are in need of mental-health services; for example, studies have generally found that about 15% of older people living in the community have significant depressive symptoms (Hinrichsen, 1990). However, there is a serious underutilization of mental-health services by this segment of the population. When older people do seek services, they tend not to receive the same diagnoses and treatments as younger people with the same symptoms. A number of authors have researched this phenomenon throughout the health-care field. One consistent finding is that health-care professionals tend to hold negative stereotypical attitudes towards elderly patients, often preferring not to work with them at all (Ahmed, Kraft, & Porter, 1987).

In a classic study, Ford and Sbordone (1980) presented 179 psychiatrists with questionnaires regarding four clinical vignettes. The results showed that the psychiatrists tended to evaluate elderly patients as less "ideal" (i.e., as less desirable patients to work with) than younger patients with exactly the same histories and symptoms. Similar results have been found with other mental-health professionals: negative attitudes affect the type, extent, and quality of mental-health care received.

These biases are not limited to mental-health care. They exist in virtually all of the health-care professions. Physical therapists and dentists, for instance, may provide less aggressive forms of intervention and may have lower standards of care for their elderly patients than they have for their younger patients.

An unfortunate consequence of ageism is that the elderly often collaborate with the people who discriminate against them. They may also believe that their diseases or symptoms are an inevitable part of aging. If they are treated as "less desirable" patients or useless human beings, it becomes a *self-fulfilling prophecy*. Adopting society's negative stereotypes as their own, many old people lose the motivation and self-esteem necessary to seek adequate treatment and rehabilitation.

A sad commentary on the effect of ageism is the uncovering, beginning in the 1970s, of the existence of *elder abuse*, and the increase in reports since then. Negative attitudes that dehumanize the elderly make it easier for the abuser to commit the crime.

The New Ageism

Palmore (1990) has introduced the concept of positive ageism to indicate prejudice and discrimination *in favor of* the aged. Ageism, as described above, is still present, but the last decade has witnessed a great deal of improvement. Generally, attitudes towards the aged are warmer. Programs dedicated to the social, mental, and physical well-being of seniors have been developed and are operating successfully all over the country. Businesses extend discounts, and governments at all levels offer tax breaks and other entitlements to the elderly.

New ageism, a term coined by Kalish (1979), is a reaction to the improved economic status of the elderly, which is perceived as "progress on the backs of the younger generation." The best way to understand the enviousness and fear behind new ageism is to consider the following:

1. People 65 and over are the most rapidly growing segment of American society—31,241,831 (12.6% of the population) in 1990 (U.S. Bureau of Census, 1990), and an estimated 64.6 million (21.8% of the population) in 2030 (U.S. Bureau of Census, 1989).
2. The median income of those over 65 has risen more than that of any other age group. This is due in part to tax-supported entitlements.
3. Federal outlays for the elderly represent one-third of total federal expenditures (Laurie, 1987). In 1986, Medicare cost the federal government $64 billion. Social Security and veterans' compensation benefits cost $182 billion (U.S. Senate Special Committee on Aging, 1988).

Thus, a number of people fear that by the time they become eligible for benefits, the system—overburdened by the huge number of recipients—will be bankrupt. The "new old" will be left "holding the bag," despite the fact that they contributed to the system throughout their entire working lives. In response, Butler (1989) claims that this notion of impending Social Security bankruptcy is not a reality. He claims that the system is building huge surpluses to compensate for the future situation—namely, relatively low numbers of workers making Social Security payments and relatively large numbers of retirees receiving benefits. On the other hand, some people insist that those surpluses are being borrowed to offset the federal deficit, and the money could disappear by the time the younger generation is old enough to collect it (Beck, 1990). Fortunately, this resentment and fear is not widespread. However, it is too early to tell what impact such ideas will have on prejudice and discrimination toward the elderly in the future.

THE INNER EXPERIENCE OF AGING

The external experience of aging (e.g., wrinkles, graying hair, diminished strength) is obvious. The "context of aging"—that is, the consequences of stereotyping and discrimination in an ageist society—takes a keener eye to detect. Even more difficult to discern is the *inner experience* of aging. Most of us do not even consider that, because of their maturity, older people may have a qualitatively different inner experience from that of other groups of adults.

We have no trouble understanding that the very young have age-related motivations, goals, fears, and distinctive ways of perceiving the world. For example, preschoolers have no trouble with logical inconsistencies. Seeing multiple Santas while Christmas shopping does not detract from their belief in Santa Claus. They fear monsters under the bed, even though they can see that nothing is there. Children have little capacity for taking the perspective of another person, and their moral reasoning is generally driven by the pursuit of pleasure and the avoidance of punishment. Later it is driven by the desire to have others "like" them, and still later by a rigid ethic based on social order (Kohlberg, 1976).

Unfortunately, fine discriminations in the adult "inner world" have received less attention. Loevinger's work on ego development is a notable exception (Loevinger, 1976). Loevinger describes a 10-stage continuum of internal perceptions about one's self and others, a continuum that individuals traverse during their lifetimes. In the last two stages (rarely attained by people who are not old), individuals possess a greater understanding of their own dynamics and are much more self-accepting than they were earlier in life. People in this stage are able to reconcile their inner conflicts. In the final stage, they mentally let go of the unattainable. Furthermore, instead of merely tolerating differences in others, they actually cherish those differences. Since they no longer seek external definitions of who they are or who they should be, they explore their own individuality with a degree of comfort and security (see Chapter 4, Table 4.3).

Many other aspects of the inner world—such as dreaming, imaging, fantasizing, meditating, creating, loving, grieving, and dying—have been neglected (Kastenbaum, 1973). For the most part, therefore, we do not have a grasp on the phenomenology of aging. We are not familiar with the goals, fears, and concerns of older people. We are more in touch with the motivations, values, and needs of youth—in part because we can recall some of them. Old age is yet to come, and thus is an unknown. However, if we are to construct an accurate model of normal aging and plan for the dramatic increase in the older population, it behooves us to study these inner experiences.

One aspect of the inner experience that has received some attention is the tendency for older people to reminisce. Highlighted introspection and reflection and excessive recounting of the past—often to the dismay of others—seem to be universal and timeless (Birren, 1964).

I remember an elderly great uncle whom I saw but once a year at the traditional Thanksgiving dinner at my sister-in-law's house. Uncle Fred was both admired and avoided. At age 80, the former house-painter still did small favors for relatives, painting their front doors, mantels, or stair railings. Everyone thought he was remarkable for his good health, warm personality, and generosity. However, no one wanted to sit next to him. No sooner had the turkey been carved than Uncle Fred began to recount his youth to the relatives on his left and right. Often the anecdotes were accompanied by his renditions of World War I marching songs and romantic ballads of the same period.

Butler (1963) writes about the common but curious phenomenon of *mirror gazing*, in which elderly people (catching their reflections in the mirror) are propelled into a course of preoccupation with past deeds. For example, I know about one woman who, since the recent death of her husband, has spent much of her time reflecting on her life as a wife and mother.

Unless they understand that such reminiscing is a normal part of the inner experience of aging, younger people often perceive it—at best—as an annoying and unfortunate consequence of old age or—at worst—as a sign of dementia and "the beginning of the end." Butler (1963) believes that this "looking back" over one's life is stimulated by the proximity of death. It helps the older person recast painful past events so that they will no longer cause despair. Uncle Fred's stories help him to relive his former "greatness" in the face of the many losses of old age. The wife and mother can, in her reflections, resolve old conflicts and enjoy her later years with renewed energy.

Mental-health professionals, armed with an understanding of this normal process, are effectively using *life review* as a therapeutic technique to help depressed elderly persons restore positive self-images, affirm their self-identity, and release grief (Butler, 1980; Viney, Benjamin, & Preston, 1989).

One suspects that as the population ages, more and more attention will turn to uncovering age-related inner phenomena and characteristics in the aged. The advertising industry, aware of the "graying" of the marketplace, is already exploring the older adult mind so that products and advertising will have optimal appeal for this potential market. In the 1990s, Madison Avenue is much less likely to produce ads depicting an older person snoozing in a rocking chair or being forgetful and confused. Instead, advertisers are increasingly focusing on discovering what makes older people tick—the better to appeal to their discretionary dollars. Recently, this market has been tagged with acronyms like GUMPIES (grown-up mature people), RAPPIES (retired affluent professionals), and the "golden MAFIA" (mature, active, free, indulgent, affluent) (Polman, 1989).

STUDYING THE ELDERLY

There are special problems and considerations inherent in studying the elderly. First, of course, is defining what we mean by "old." Although the cutoff point seems to be inching further away, old age is still considered to refer to those 65 and older. Nevertheless, because of the subjectiveness and relativity of the concept of age, many of the "aged" may not see themselves as old (Covey, 1985). Negative stereotyping and consequent self-hatred may cause people to deny that they are old and may make them unwilling to participate in *gerontological research*. On the other hand, identifying subjects as old may make them act in what they perceive as "age-appropriate" ways, rather than merely behaving naturally.

Second, the researcher must be especially sensitive to situations and events such as chronic illness or recent loss that might influence the elderly subject's responses. Hunger, fatigue, or medications may also induce temporary mental decline or confusion in some elderly research subjects.

Next, a number of ethical issues must be weighed. The majority of elderly subjects in most research projects have been *convenience samples*—that is, they have been residents of institutions such as nursing homes or mental hospitals. Not only are such samples nonrepresentative (only 5% of the elderly live in institutions), but also institutionalized subjects may be dependent on the services provided by the institution and may thus feel compelled to cooperate. Older people living with family members might not feel free to comment honestly for fear of offending the relatives who support them (Keith, 1980).

Finally, older people often excel in traits and attributes that are exceedingly difficult to study in a systematic way. Orchestral conductors, composers, diplomats, and statesmen often reach their professional peaks in their 60s, 70s, and 80s, but we have yet to develop adequate *instruments* to measure such constructs as creativity and wisdom (J. E. Birren, personal communication, 1990).

ASPIRATIONS IN THE LATER YEARS

The importance of understanding the inner experience of aging is eloquently expressed by Kaufman (1986):

In order to improve the quality of life experience for those in their later years, we must understand what it means to be at the end of a life cycle and have 70 or more years of experience on which to reflect. For only by first knowing how the elderly view themselves, their lives, and the nature of old age can we hope to fashion a meaningful present and future for them and for those that follow. (p. 4)

If one can learn about people from accounts of their past, then surely one can also learn about people from listening to them talk about their future. Personal goals, dreams, fantasies, and ambitions are incredibly revealing. This book will attempt to present a more balanced picture of normal aging by exploring the *aspirations* of a group of elderly people living in a relatively "ideal" situation, one that protects them from many of the obstacles (e.g., inadequate housing, poor health care) and other forms of discrimination that preoccupy their peers and prevent them from reaching their late-life potential.

Aspirations are desires to achieve personal goals in the near future ("I want to see my new grandchild this coming spring"), the distant future (from a 75-year-old man, "I want to live to be 100 like my father"), or in an indeterminate future ("Before I die, I want to learn how to weave"). Although an aspiration exists in the present, it can be a few moments old or it could have its roots in childhood dreams. Aspirations, with their links to the past, present, and future, are wonderful vehicles to illuminate the inner experience of the aged.

Methodology

There are three major ways of conducting research: a *quantitative* approach, a *qualitative* approach, or a combination of both. Quantitative methods seek facts or causes, express data numerically, and rely on statistical analyses (e.g., *tests of significance*). The aim is to predict and control phenomena. Qualitative methods, on the other hand, are based on linguistic data, either written or verbal. The purpose is to understand human meaning and experience. Sometimes both approaches are used in the same study. Demographic data may be included in qualitative studies. Similarly, selected case studies or interviews may be incorporated into quantitative studies to highlight certain aspects of the topic.

One of the tenets of the *human science approach* (another name for qualitative research) is that the subject matter under study should determine the method used, rather than the other way around (Thomas, 1989). Exploring the aspirations of the elderly requires a method that permits entry into the subjective world of older people. *Ethnography* (also called field research or community study) is a method that allows for such intimacy. It encompasses three techniques—*in-depth interview*, the *case study*, and *participant-observation*.

I chose the participant-observation technique to study aspirations, which means that during the period of *data collection* I lived in Franklin Village (a retirement community) and participated in the daily life of the community. My participation became my research tool. As Keith (1980) writes, "The observer's personal involvement in a research setting is always a central means to understand it . . . rather than using a research instrument, the participant-observer becomes one" (p. 9).

In order to obtain *informants* for my study, I used *snowball sampling*. This means that I was introduced to a few residents who then introduced me to others who then referred me to still more residents. Eventually, this technique led me to 81 residents who were willing to share their aspirations with me.

Some residents I met only once, while others became regular informants. I used no tape recorders or notebooks during the prearranged interviews or the informal chats that occurred by chance. Such devices tend to make people self-conscious by reminding them that they are being observed and studied. I also did not want to be dependent on anything that could malfunction or distract me from noticing nonverbal communication or my surroundings.

At first, I was concerned that I would forget important statements, enlightening quotes, and meaningful behaviors. However, I developed an uncanny ability for recall. Immediately after an interaction, I would rush to a secluded spot—my room, a shady tree along the border of the community, or, in a pinch, my car. There I would furiously jot down key words and phrases of all I had seen and heard. I took special care in noting verbatim any expressions of aspirations. Often I would write down my thoughts on the research methodology or anything else (insightful or trivial) that came to mind. I always kept Keith's (1980) phrase in mind: "If it is not written down, it never happened" (p. 53).

At the end of each day, I reconstructed and dictated every event and description in my notebook into a tape recorder. In the morning, I mailed the cassette to an assistant who immediately transcribed the tapes and sent back the data in typewritten logs. The period of time between the beginning and end of this process was usually no more than four days. After reading the typewritten logs, I would frequently notice incomplete information or vague remarks that would send me back to the participants for clarification.

That was the easy part. The hard part came after the data-gathering phase was complete and I left the community. I had 352 typewritten pages of narrative to analyze. I immersed myself in the data, reading and rereading the logs.

After countless readings over many months, I noticed that common themes began to emerge. The residents of Franklin Village seemed to place great importance on their relationships with others. They expressed wishes to help friends and family, and they desired intimate social contact. The residents often referred to the ways in which they wanted to live their last days, including how they would like to die.

The aspirations I collected were not merely unrelated idle thoughts or musings. They were often expressed with emotional intensity and conviction, and most of them were in process— that is, the residents were working on achieving them. I went through many rounds of *content analysis*, finally organizing the

TABLE 1.1
Aspirations and the Values that Motivate Them (Franklin Village)

Values	Aspirations (N = 240)
Autonomy N = 65 (27%)	- A good death (quick, easy) - Choice - Independence (not be a burden) - Longevity - Mental health - Physical health
Personal Growth N = 55 (23%)	- Awareness of events (well-informed) - Ideal traits (e.g., intelligence, courage, patience) - Insight - New experiences - New knowledge (learning) - Spiritual self-improvement
Helping N = 35 (14.5%)	- Affect social change - Help others
Social Ties N = 33 (13.5%)	- Family harmony - Family survival - Family unity - Intimate contact (family, friends, staff)
Pleasure N = 52 (22%)	- Activity (e.g., sports) - Aesthetics (beauty and order) - Complete tasks - Creative work - Maintain the status quo (life-style) - Re-create past experiences - Relaxation

data into five major groups. The importance of the aspirations—the emotion and conviction as well as the behavior connected with many of them—helped me to understand that these aspirations were driven by *values* (personal beliefs that motivate action). Table 1.1 depicts the five major values that I encountered at Franklin Village and examples of the aspirations that derived from each one of them.

Twenty-seven percent of the statements about aspirations reflected the residents' high regard for personal *autonomy*. Another 23% indicated the importance of *personal growth*, which stimulated desires for spiritual and intellectual self-improvement. *Helping*, or altruism, was still another value that motivated nearly 15% of the aspirations; this value included wishes to serve others and to promote social change.

Goals involving the well-being of friends and family members were frequent. Approximately 14% of the aspirations expressed at Franklin Village grew out of this value, which I called *social ties*. Finally, 22% of the statements were rooted in the high regard for *pleasure* in the later years.

The next chapter will describe my "adventures" in Franklin Village, how I convinced the *gatekeepers* to let me in, and the wonderful residents who became my friends and, incidentally, the subjects of my research. I spent 1,000 hours talking to the residents of Franklin Village, inside their apartments, along the paths that connected the clusters of apartments, and on benches under trees. Sometimes I chatted with those in wheelchairs or beds. Many pleasant hours were spent in the weaving room, the carpentry shop, and the lounges. Every encounter provided a glimpse into the inner experience of aging.

CHAPTER 2

FRANKLIN VILLAGE

"Up close and personal"

Franklin Village,* a community of 722 elderly people, is built on the site of what was once a large farm, with rolling green hills and picturesque ponds. The restored 200-year-old stone farmhouse, with fireplaces in each room, serves as a cozy guest house for visitors.

The population of Franklin Village is diverse. The ages of the residents range from 65 to 103. Residents live in houses, apartments, and single rooms. Some people are spry and healthy; others are frail and feeble. Some are gregarious and easy to befriend, whereas others are reclusive. What they all had in common, I believed, was that, in a seemingly Utopian setting like Franklin Village, they would want for little. Was I assuming too much?

Franklin Village is a *continuing care retirement community* (CCRC), a form of long-term care that has become popular during the past 20 years. Residents pay an entrance fee, plus a monthly service fee that entitles them to a modern, attractive apartment, meals, and a range of health-care and social services, including recreation, maintenance of their home and appliances, and skilled nursing care when needed. Should a resident become too disabled to live independently, a nursing home within the community is the next step.

---

*To protect the privacy of the community and its residents, all names and certain identifying characteristics have been changed.

The setting supports independence and autonomy. Residents do housekeeping only if they choose. Medical care is available without an appointment. Residents socialize as much or as little as they want. The community is removed from the dangers of the city, but it is near enough for regular shuttles into town for shopping or entertainment. Residents can keep their cars if they are still driving. However, if they wish, they can do nothing but enjoy the comforts of staying at home.

Franklin Village is open to everyone, but it is owned and operated by the Religious Order of Friends (more commonly known as Quakers). One-third of the residents are Quakers.

Some years before I had even heard about Franklin Village, I had been inspired by the book, *Number Our Days*, in which Barbara Myerhoff, a young anthropologist, described how she entered and befriended a community of elderly Jews in Southern California (Myerhoff, 1978). The lives of these elderly Jewish immigrants were full of hardship and pain. Myerhoff spent hundreds of hours talking with these older people in their rundown Venice Beach Senior Center and in their modest homes. What she was able to communicate to her readers was not merely the pain and suffering of age but also the remarkable capacity of the human spirit to survive.

I knew that if I wanted to learn about aging, I would have to follow Barbara Myerhoff's example—in other words, as they say on television sports programs, to get "up close and personal." Other researchers have "entered" communities of old people, but as far as I knew no one had studied old people in a privileged environment like Franklin Village. I felt that Franklin Village would give me the opportunity to study elderly people who did not have many of the usual obstacles discussed earlier. Once I discovered Franklin Village, I had to convince the community to allow me to "move in," so that I could become a participant-observer.

ENTRY INTO THE COMMUNITY

My requests were simple. I wanted to live in Franklin Village during my three-month summer hiatus from college teaching. I knew that there was a guest house on the grounds, but the daily rates would be more than I could afford. I hoped for a guest-house discount or the sofa-bed of a kindly resident. I wanted permission to eat with residents in the dining hall and coffee shop, to participate in recreational activities and social gatherings, and to move freely about the community.

No one could guarantee that people would share their innermost thoughts and feelings. But if they did, I wanted permission to record and communicate that personal information beyond the community (first in a doctoral thesis and later, I hoped, in a book) so that others could gain insight about the experience of aging. Most of all, I just wanted a bed to sleep in and the freedom to become a member of the community. I assumed that the rest would come naturally if I was a good neighbor and friend.

For months I met with the gatekeepers—board members, administrators, and residents. Dr. Thomas, an alumnus of my university, was my first and staunchest supporter. The first of many meetings took place in Dr. Thomas's office, along with two other administrators.

The first roadblock surfaced moments into the meeting. The administrators said that, if I got the permission I requested, I would have to use *consent forms* to protect the confidentiality and privacy of the residents. These forms would be formal agreements signed by residents that would document their consent to use the content of our conversations for research purposes. I was caught in a dilemma. Asking residents to sign a consent form before they got to know me might create barriers and suspicion. I suggested instead that a group of residents monitor my movement through the community to observe whether I was intruding on residents' privacy. For the moment, the issue was dropped.

The months of preliminary meetings were difficult. I wanted

to conduct the study so much that at times I felt that I would promise anything just to "get in." At other times, I felt defensive or angry at their "pickiness" and was fearful that I might "blow it." I tried to hold my emotions in check, especially my bubbling enthusiasm, which I thought might be misperceived.

The second meeting was the most anxiety-provoking. It should have been a "piece of cake" because it consisted of residents, not administrators, and was held in the comfortable "simple Quaker elegance" of the restored farmhouse. Unfortunately, I was held up by traffic and arrived late. Thirty-five pairs of eyes watched as I awkwardly took a seat. I barely had a moment to relax when I was asked to give my presentation. After my talk, there were several questions. One older woman, sitting on a Victorian love seat and looking lovely and Victorian herself, asked if I was going to be conducting a similar study in another setting.

I had two thoughts—first, that these residents would keep me on my toes, and second, that I would have to be honest in my responses. She was, of course, thinking about the value of the findings of the proposed study. How could a study about people living a comfortable old age be useful, since most elderly people do not have similar living situations? I shared my belief that this situation might provide a view of how the experience of old age "could be" under optimal conditions—important information if we are to understand the parameters of *normal aging*.

Another woman wanted to know if I would be asking many questions. Apparently, other researchers had come into the community in the past, armed with questionnaires and surveys. She wanted assurance that my study was not going to be more of the same. After hearing that I wanted to live in the community, one resident commented that perhaps I wouldn't mind joining one of the 63 resident committees.

A few weeks after this meeting, the *Institutional Review Board* met to discuss my proposal. This group is composed of members of the board of directors, administrators, and residents. I was not invited. Unfortunately, this group had serious reservations about my proposed study. I was downhearted when Dr. Thomas told me that they did not grant approval—but they did not deny it, either.

Dr. Thomas and I met to discuss the group's reservations and prepare responses. I was invited to the next Institutional Review Board meeting, at which time the board would grant or deny access—and, if access were granted, would specify the ground rules. I felt a growing panic. I had already begun my summer break. The research was scheduled to begin in a week, and I had yet to receive approval. I was very discouraged. Early on, Dr. Thomas warned me that decisions at the community were made in "Quaker fashion"—that is, by consensus, and slowly.* Meanwhile, time was running out. There were no provisions for delay. I had to resume teaching in the fall.

The consent form was still an issue. My residence in the community was an even bigger issue. Certain members of the Institutional Review Board felt that it was "inappropriate" for me to live there. Anything more than one or two nights a week, in their view, would create a "fish bowl" situation for the residents. They might be uncomfortable to be under constant observation. I was distraught. How could I develop the closeness I wanted? How could I manage the three-hour commute from my home?

Finally, the day of the final Institutional Review Board meeting arrived. I wanted to be perceived as a sincere person, so I began my presentation by relating the wonderful childhood experience of sharing a bedroom with my grandmother. Although the anecdote was true, I realized that it was not working. The ploy was too obvious, so I tried to relax and be myself.

The consent-form issue arose early. Fortunately, one of the

---

*In a Quaker "business meeting," one dissenting person can hold up the action. Certain "weighty" members (members who, by the nature of their experience and knowledge, know more about the issues at hand) are very influential. If people do not agree, but do not want to impede the process, they will "step aside." This means that they will not object to the discussion and that consensus will be obtained.

members of the board, who had not been present at the previous meeting, spoke in my behalf. Dr. King, an anthropologist and gerontological researcher, said that my "whipping out" a consent form in the midst of casual conversation would alarm people, perhaps inhibiting them and causing concern where none existed before. The committee finally agreed that I should present the consent form only after lengthy formal interviews. Casual conversations would not require the forms. Another one of the members turned to me and asked, "Are you comfortable with that?" The process had been an example of a Quaker business meeting and of Quaker decision-making. Everyone "needs to be comfortable" with a decision.

Other issues of how I would identify myself and of informing residents about my arrival to the community were taken care of quickly. Then I was asked to leave the room while they resolved any lingering issues—the most important of which, of course, was my residence in the community.

I left the room feeling relieved and optimistic. It occurred to me that my experience was probably not unlike the experience of potential residents, who must go through a series of meetings with administrators and residents to demonstrate that they will "fit" and not cause problems in the community. There seemed to be a paradox. Although the community is founded on the principle of individual autonomy and self-determination, the administration goes to great lengths to "protect" the residents.

Twenty minutes later, Dr. Thomas came out to deliver the good news. The committee decided to give me free rein. I could stay at the guest house as often as I wanted, at no charge. I would be permitted to eat my meals in the coffee shop or dining hall. Every two weeks I would receive a bill for my meals. And Dr. King, who had spoken so forcefully in my behalf, was to be my advisor. I had survived my rite of passage and was ready to begin.

THE COMMUNITY

Franklin Village is bordered by ponds, a three-hole golf course, vegetable gardens, and a berry patch. Small parking areas are sprinkled throughout the community and along its edges. A 1 1/2 mile-long path around the perimeter of the community is used by some residents for early-morning walks.

The "Center" is where most socialization takes place, including cultural, educational, and entertainment activities. It is a long, rectangular building (first floor and lower level) with a main entrance in the middle and several other entranceways at the sides and in the back. It houses the coffee shop, the dining room, the library, and an auditorium for concerts and special programs. The Franklin Village administrative offices are also located at the Center, as are the residents' mailboxes. Most committee meetings are held in rooms on the lower level.

The Center also contains the medical facility, which provides all levels of nursing care, physical therapy, and outpatient services. The halls are wide enough for the motorized "buggies" (resembling golf carts) that some residents use. In a sense, the Center serves as an *objective measure* for residents' mobility. If residents can make a daily trip to the Center, either on foot or by buggies, they are considered able enough to maintain independent apartments. When the trip becomes too difficult, it is considered time for them to move into the Center to occupy a one-room apartment, either in the limited-nursing facility or the around-the-clock nursing area. No one, however, makes that decision for the resident. Residents eventually realize that when going to the Center requires more energy or strength than they can muster, it is best to "go under the roof."

People dress up to come to the Center, especially for the evening meal. Housedresses, pants for the women, or shorts are rarely seen. At dinner, men wear jackets, and women wear their best clothes.

The atmosphere resembles a resort. A receptionist, who seems to know every resident, greets each one with a smile and a few words as they enter the building. Residents can buy the *New York Times* at the front desk or borrow from a selection of local newspapers. Residents bring their old newspapers and aluminum cans to the Center to be recycled.

On the first floor, there is a resident-run gift shop. The merchandise is purchased by residents, displayed by residents, sold by residents. Volunteer clerks work two-hour shifts. They have regular work schedules and regard their shift at the gift shop to be a job, even though they are not paid. The merchandise is geared towards an older population. Greeting cards are conservative. There are items (such as clothes and toys) that one could purchase for visiting grandchildren or send to grandchildren of all ages. Costume jewelry and clothing are also geared to the taste of an older population, especially women. There is a wide assortment of drugstore items, including stationery and postcards.

Across from the gift shop is the coffee shop, where residents dine informally. The coffee shop also sells basic groceries (milk, eggs, bread, juice, etc.) for the residents' small kitchens. Many residents prefer to eat in the coffee shop because there are no "steady" seating arrangements there. People tend not to make prearranged "dates" to eat in the coffee shop. Instead, they join others spontaneously at the front door or walkway on their way to the Center. Staff members also eat in the coffee shop, although not at the same tables. The coffee shop became one of my favorite places to meet people. It is often crowded, which means that people who don't know each other share tables.

This is not the case in the adjacent dining room, where people will prearrange table seating—sometimes days or weeks ahead. If someone goes into the dining room without a "date," the hostess asks if he or she would like to sit at a table with others. If so, the hostess approaches a table and asks if the diners would like to have the resident join them. The newcomer and the occupants of the table may—and sometimes do—decline.

The high ceilings of the dining room create an airy atmosphere. From almost anywhere in the room, one can see the green rolling hills outside the many large picture windows. Youthful waiters and waitresses and clean-up people are friendly and polite. They all seem familiar with the habits of residents. For instance, they will ask, "Would you like your regular breakfast?" or "Would you like your tea now?" Certain tables are "closed" tables—that is, the same people dine together for years and years. Other tables are semiclosed. In this case, there is a core of people who generally sit together, with several "floaters" (people who prefer to change tables frequently).

To the left of the coffee shop is the entrance to the nursing-care facilities. They are neither hospitals nor nursing homes. Nurses and doctors wear their regular street clothes. The hallways and rooms are carpeted, which means that there is less clatter and less hospital-type noise. Wide corridors give a spacious, open-air feeling. There is an absence of the usual smells found in medical settings. Still, one is acutely aware that the patients are very old and frail.

In the center of the building, along the wall, are residents' mailboxes and a large bulletin board that displays the schedule of events for the week, announcements about new staff members, transportation schedules, and memorials for residents who have died during that month. The memorials announce the date of the death and the location of the memorial service.

The Center is a quiet place. Even at mealtimes, when people spill into the corridors, it is never crowded. The hallways are frequently adorned with artwork by local artists or by Franklin Village artists. Vases of flowers are placed on tables along the main hallways. The Flower-Arranging Committee (one of many resident-initiated committees) creates, places, and maintains the arrangements.

Antique tables, sofas and chairs in traditional or Victorian style also line the wide hallways. Most of this furniture is donated by residents who moved from independent apartments into the nursing-care facilities. (The move to smaller quarters usually requires residents to dispose of many possessions.) The same style of elegance and fine furniture is in the sitting-room across from the dining room. A 1,000-piece puzzle sits on a large table. Passers-by (residents, staff members, or visitors) frequently stop to work on it for a few minutes before moving on. When the puzzle is finished, it remains on display for a few days— until someone comes along, takes it apart, and begins a new one.

The library is down the hall from the dining room. Most of the books are donated by the residents. The selection is so large that the overflow is housed in extra bookcases in the hallway. Resident volunteers work in the library; many are retired librarians. The Quaker meeting is held there every Sunday.

Activity rooms are on the lower level. Colorful travel posters line the walls of the game room, which has a Ping-Pong table, a billiard table, and a shuffleboardlike table game. The English lawn-bowling game covers half of the floor space. Like most of the activity rooms, the game room is used primarily in the morning. (After lunch, many residents return to their apartments to rest or nap.) Most mornings, one can find the men engaged in a lot of good-natured joking and teasing while they compete in English lawn-bowling. Once a week, the women play.

A well-equipped workshop is next to the game room. Most of the tools are donated by residents who no longer have space for private workshops. Men build furniture, shelves, and small knickknacks. They repair the furniture, jewelry, shoes, and belts of the other residents. The fees collected are "voluntary"; residents decide what they think the work is worth. That money goes into a kitty to be used for entertainment, recreational, and educational events. Like the game room, the workshop is busiest in the morning.

The Center also houses rooms for ceramics and pottery, with a kiln for firing. A weaving room and a sewing room (which is used primarily for quilting) are on the lower level.

Walking into the beauty shop on the lower level is like walking backwards in time. It reminded me of the beauty shops my mother used to take me to when I was a child. There are rows of old-fashioned hair dryers; the women sitting under them are reading magazines. There are no signs of the hair blowers, mousses, or other current fashionable tools of the trade. It is not uncommon to see an attendant wheeling in someone from the nursing facilities. Everyone understands the therapeutic value of a shampoo and set.

Near the beauty shop are four large display cases that hold many of the prized possessions of residents. The Display Case Committee "puts out a monthly call" for personal treasures that fit a changing theme (e.g., "the Far East," or "cold weather"). The committee arranges the items in the cases for all to admire until they are returned to their owners at the end of the month.

From the Center, one can walk outdoors from either the lower or the first-floor level. Covered walkways connect the Center to all of the apartment clusters. The clusters consist of as many as five or six apartments, or as few as two. Most clusters, however, consist of three or four apartments. The outside walls are constructed of rustic silver-gray weathered wood. Residents are encouraged to decorate their doorways. Interesting doormats, hanging chimes, small sculptures and pottery, or hanging baskets of flowers and plants enhance most doorways.

Well-manicured gardens, plants, shrubs, and trees surround each cluster. Most of the trees are labeled with their common and botanical names on green plastic tags. It is not uncommon to see a resident bend down to pull a weed as he or she walks along the path to the Center.

In the daylight hours, service people can be seen along the walkways and entering the apartments. Some are cleaning the apartments or servicing appliances; others are cutting grass or pruning shrubs. Residents and maintenance people greet each other with cheery hellos. Altogether, the atmosphere is one of courteousness, cheerfulness, and a genuine pride and interest in the upkeep of the community.

Within the community is a mini-community of 18 full-size houses. Residents who occupy these homes do not receive meals at the Center, nor are they eligible for the wide spectrum of medical-care services provided for the other residents. However, they do receive cleaning and maintenance services. People who choose this arrangement are, on average, younger than most residents. They want, at least initially, a more independent life. But they are fully aware that this house is not their final home. They too, as they age, will have to move into the apartments with full services and perhaps eventually into the nursing facilities.

Close to the Center is the 200-year-old farmhouse turned guest house that would be my home. The first floor has a living room, dining room, sitting room, and kitchen. The upper floor has six guest rooms. Behind the guest house is a swimming pool used by residents and guests. Next to the pool area is a spot that is secluded by large old shade trees—a place that was to become the sanctuary where I would sort my feelings and record my thoughts into my tape recorder.

ASPIRATIONS AND VALUES

My arrival was announced on the bulletin board, in the community newspaper, and at several community meetings. I also wore a large green badge that identified me—in the oversized letters requested by the Board.

Dr. Thomas introduced me to Hubert and Beth, two residents who were to become my friends and confidants. Hubert and Beth introduced me to their friends, who in turn introduced me to their friends. Before long, I was invited to tea, committee meetings, and the Quaker Sunday Meeting. Other residents approached me spontaneously.

Whenever I met someone on the walkway, in the dining room, or in the activity rooms, I identified myself as a researcher studying older people's aspirations. Residents were friendly, although they seemed to be uncomfortable with the notion of aspirations. Hubert, a retired teacher, helped me with that problem. He said, "Aspiration is not a good term for old people. It sounds idealized and lofty. It's a young people's term. You need to ask old people about their goals, plans, and priorities, or simply, 'What are you going to do with the rest of your life?'" I followed his advice, and it worked. Hubert also said that people would be more comfortable if I identified myself as a student rather than a researcher. Again, I followed his advice.

The women liked Hubert, He was a handsome man at 77, tall and well-built. He was the author of dozens of Quaker publications. Hubert frequently gave me advice—for instance, "Don't you think that you are talking to too many women or too many Quakers or too many healthy people?" That comment sent me scurrying about, looking for men, Protestants, and ill or disabled people. Hubert's comment also caused me to seek out the less articulate, less popular residents, as well as other "different" residents. Although the 81 elderly people I came to know did not represent a *random* sample, they were a diverse group, thanks to Hubert.

If I were to learn about the inner experience of aging, in even such a privileged place as Franklin Village, Hubert said that I would have to ask about frustrations as well as aspirations. Even Hubert, with his popularity, accomplishments, and obvious vitality, had frustrations. "Many talented older people," he said, "are left unwanted and unused because of the belief that old people are useless, feeble, and not worth much socially and intellectually. I for one [here his face reddened] do not experience myself as an old man. I have a lot to offer." In the past, Hubert had given hundreds of speeches, but no one calls any more. He asked a few local elementary school principals if they would like him to bring his international collection of hats to a school assembly and give a talk about the countries they came from. The lack of response hurt. Except for this frustration, Hubert appears happy. On Sunday he has dinner in the dining room with his two brothers and their wives—also residents. (Hubert never married.) Other times, he prefers the informality of the coffee shop.

Dr. Thomas introduced me to Beth because she was such an outgoing woman. She was one of the earliest residents of Franklin Village and seemed to know everyone. Every Friday, Beth and another woman dressed in clown outfits and spent the morning cheering up nursing-care patients with their funny made-up faces and clever antics. She carried gold stars in her pocket. If people "seemed to need it," Beth put a gold star on the back of their hands, gave them a big hug, and told them how much she liked them.

My presence gave Beth another aspiration besides her aspiration to clown—that is, she wanted to help me meet residents and to feel at home. Beth would invite me to have dinner with her and, lo and behold, there would be 10 other people at the table. She held nonalcoholic Happy Hours in her apartment, where I would meet still more new faces.

Helping me and cheering the sick made Beth feel good. Most residents, including Hubert and Beth, actively sought such opportunities. The ethic of altruism at Franklin Village suggests that helping may be an important value, not only in this community but among this age group in general. Although we are aware that some values may be culturally, religiously, gender, or class-based, we are less familiar with those that are age-related. The age-related values that we do recognize usually concern younger populations. For example, most young people highly value physical appearance. It is often the deciding factor in choosing dates or mates. Inordinate amounts of time and money are spent in enhancing "looks." Power and acquisition of goods and money, on the other hand, are often associated with middle adulthood. The cohort effect may contribute to value differences between the generations. Older people, for instance, may value family ties more than younger people because the older generation was *socialized* when family ties were considered more important than they are today (Palmore, 1978). The cohort effect is responsible for the stereotype that older people are "old-fashioned" (Palmore, 1990). We seem, however, to know little of the values of old age.

The values of the elderly may hold clues to many important questions, such as "What is normal aging?" "What is successful aging?" and "How can we provide for our elderly population, so that they will enjoy meaningful lives until the end of life itself?"

They may also provide a lens through which we can better understand the inner experience of aging.

The next five chapters of the book will address the values that I found at Franklin Village—values that I believe are characteristic of the elderly. These values go beyond mere survival; they include autonomy, personal growth, helping, social ties, and pleasure. They are the foundation for the hundreds of aspirations that the residents of Franklin Village shared with me.

PART II

ASPIRATIONS

CHAPTER 3

AUTONOMY

"Having tea or ice cream whenever you like"

INDEPENDENCE

When Lily woke up, it was dark in her room, but images from her dream were still vivid. She saw herself sitting on the porch swing with her beau, Spencer, who reached into his pocket and pulled out a small black velvet box. He opened it slowly, savoring her surprise, just like he had in real life 75 years before. Inside the box was a sparkling diamond, set on a band of white gold. She had never seen anything so beautiful in all of Fairview County. In the dream, Spencer asked, "Will you marry me?" This time, Lily said, "Yes."

Now fully awake, Lily sighed and reached for the water glass, only to find that she had forgotten to refill it before going to bed. Pushing the light blanket aside brought her no relief from the humid night. "Maybe a drink of water will cool me off," she thought. She rose from the bed carefully, feeling the walls for guidance. Suddenly, she became disoriented. "This isn't right," she thought. Panic filled her as she groped furiously for the doorway. She stubbed her toe, then bumped into furniture. After several minutes, she dropped to her knees, exhausted. Bruised and frightened, she fell asleep on the floor. When morning came, she found herself next to the bed. She raised herself from the floor slowly and painfully.

Lily is a 98-year-old retired schoolteacher whom I met by chance on one of the covered walkways at Franklin Village. She was on her way to dinner, and I was searching for the apartment of a resident. She smiled and asked if she could help. "My name is Lily. It's easy to remember. Lily, silly Lily. That's what the boys called me when I was just a girl." Although I remembered her name, Lily never remembered my name, nor did she recognize me. Each time we met, we had to start our relationship anew.

Lily and I had many talks. Occasionally, former pupils (aged 39 to 79) visited. She talked about these "youngsters" and how she tried to help the "foreign ones" by learning their parents' language. It was not uncommon for Lily to lose her train of thought as she recounted her teaching days. Often, her thoughts would drift to Spencer and she would ask me, "Do you think I made a mistake? He was a good man, but I was still too much of a girl to marry." After a few minutes of musing, she would ask me, "Now, where were we?" I would remind her, and she would pick up the conversation precisely where she had left off, unfazed by the detour.

Mementos covered every flat surface in her apartment: a silver bowl engraved with her name and the date she retired, a hand-made candy dish from a child (who is probably a grandparent by now), and hundreds of photographs.

"Maintaining independence" is Lily's single aspiration. However, it comes with a heavy price. Tasks like washing, dressing, and walking to the Center for meals take all day to accomplish. "I don't know where the days go," she says frequently. "I don't have the strength to go to concerts or write anything more than my name. But it doesn't matter; I had the strength when I needed it."

"I will *never* go 'under the roof' [move into the nursing facility]. I will *never* give up my lovely things. I want to have tea or ice cream whenever I like."

Lily's hold on her independence is at the same time coura-geous and foolhardy. Refusing to go "under the roof" appears dangerously unreasonable, but the refusal is consistent with

Lily's values. It is more important to her to live the way she chooses than to live more safely under the roof. Lily's decision is an example of an older person's attempt to balance pain and self-determination in the final days of life (Collopy, 1990).

Variations of Lily's aspiration to "maintain independence" were spontaneously echoed by a large number of residents of Franklin Village. Although *independence* was the word most commonly used, *autonomy* may be a more accurate description. No resident of Franklin Village, regardless of age or health, was independent in the usual way we define the term—that is, not relying on something or someone else for one's existence. The residents' ability to live in individual apartments and retain the possessions that define their individuality *depends* on the services provided within the community.

Autonomy, on the other hand, suggests that even though one may rely on external resources, one has a range of choices and can govern one's own life to the extent possible. Although independence and autonomy are related, they are not synonymous. The more people depend on others for survival, however, the more restricted their choices are likely to become.

Many people believe that valuing independence in old age is a Western phenomenon. The Chinese, for example, value *filial piety* (respect for the aged) and the tradition that children will take care of their parents and older relatives (Cheung, Cho, Lum, Tang, & Yau, 1980). Independence in old age in Eastern cultures seems undesirable. Nevertheless, that does not mean that Chinese elderly have no autonomy. Wong (1979) studied a group of elderly Chinese who held positions of authority and leadership in Chinese associations and who considered themselves to be the "power elite" (p. 36). I suspect that even among the less powerful, most elderly people (regardless of culture) need and value choice, even if it means merely deciding when to have "tea or ice cream."

Social scientists recognize the significance of autonomy. Adler (1930) described the need to control one's personal environment as "an intrinsic necessity of life itself" (p. 398, cited in Langer &

Rodin, 1976). Langer & Rodin (1976) assessed the effects of enhanced personal choice on a group of nursing-home residents. They hypothesized that the debilitated condition of many nursing-home residents was in part the result of their having virtually no choice and that reintroducing choice into their lives would produce positive change.

Nursing-home residents were divided into two groups, an *experimental group* and a *control group.* The residents in the experimental group were provided with decision-making opportunities. They were asked to choose where to receive visitors (in their rooms, outdoors, in the lounge, etc.). Movies were shown on two days. They were to decide when they wished to see them, or if they wished to see them at all. Furniture in the rooms could be arranged any way they liked. They were offered house plants and were allowed to place them wherever they wanted and to water them as they felt best.

Residents in the control group, on the other hand, were not encouraged to make decisions. If they wanted to see visitors in a particular place, staff would arrange it. Staff would care for their plants. Staff would decide what night they would see the movie. In other words, the staff, not the residents, were responsible for the decisions that would affect the residents' daily lives.

Various *behavior measures* (e.g., how often residents participated in activities), *subjective measures* (e.g., how "happy" they felt), and staff ratings (e.g., how alert and active the residents appeared to be) were obtained before the experiment and three weeks after it ended. The *pre- and post-test results* showed dramatic differences. In the control group, 71% were rated as having become more debilitated, whereas 93% of the experimental group showed overall improvement. People in the latter group took more initiative and were more active, more vigorous, and more sociable than the others.

Eighteen months later, the improvements were still obvious (Rodin & Langer, 1977). More impressive, however, was that the mortality rate for the experimental group was 15%—versus 30% for the control group.

This brings us back to Lily. We may be incorrect in assuming that having her go under the roof would prolong her life. In her physical and mental condition, the nursing facility might provide her with a safer environment than an independent apartment, but that does not automatically mean that it would increase her longevity. In her view, it would certainly diminish her ability to govern her own life and thus diminish the *quality of her life*.

NOT BEING A BURDEN

Although older people value autonomy for its own sake, it is also valued because the family of an autonomous older person is likely to be free from the burden of caregiving. By the time one has reached old age, he or she has experienced or observed the heavy toll that caregiving can exact.

The Stones—Arthur (a 72-year-old retired financial consultant) and his wife, Edith (a 67-year-old homemaker)—decided to move into Franklin Village two years ago, solely on the basis of the "catastrophic and tragic experiences" they had in caring for their elderly parents.

Edith recalls, "Arthur's mother moved in with us after Arthur's father died. Pop had taken care of Mom. We didn't know about *Alzheimer's* back then. We just called it senility. It started with her forgetting things, being confused, and needing help to get dressed. By the time she came to live with us, it wasn't safe to leave her alone. Arthur was working, so it was my job to care for Mom. I felt guilty about snapping at her. I was angry and frustrated, but mostly I was depressed. It got so bad that I prayed for release."

Arthur interrupted, "It wasn't that we didn't love Mom. We did, but the strain on the family was tremendous—physically, emotionally, financially. Two years after Mom died, Edith's father had a stroke. He lived with us for nearly ten years, paralyzed and unable to speak, and needing total care. We do not want what happened to us to happen to our children," Arthur explained, "so we decided to move to Franklin Village, where we will be taken care of when we deteriorate."

Arthur and Edith do not feel that they are sacrificing their happiness. Their decision seems to be reasonable in light of their personalities and life experience. Arthur says, with pleasure, that Franklin Village reminds him of the small towns of his youth. Edith says, "My happiest days were when I was away at college. I am a kind of institutional person. That's why I am content at Franklin Village."

The wish not to be a burden to loved ones (children, siblings, nieces, and nephews) was given as the main reason for moving to a continuing-care retirement community. Residents usually voiced these comments with determination and pride because they had the foresight, discipline, and financial ability to ensure that the burden they experienced would not be suffered by their own children.

Nevertheless, their desire to protect their children and retain their autonomy was not always understood outside the community. The Stones told of friends and family who thought that it was unwise for older people to sell their homes, move to another part of the country, and "segregate" themselves from young people. Over the years, some of these friends changed their minds when they saw how happy the residents were or when they found, as years passed, that they also had difficulty maintaining their own homes, or when other friends became depleted by medical bills. Some friends persist in their objections to retirement communities. However, a 10-year waiting list to get into Franklin Village attests to the large number of older people who believe that life in a retirement community will extend their years of autonomy and ensure freedom for their children.

Most older people at Franklin Village are not preoccupied about death, but they *are* concerned about the way in which they live the last years or days of their lives. Rachel, a 76-year-old homemaker, and her husband Paul, an 89-year-old retired engineer, feel that they have found a solution. I sat in their living room, admiring the white crocheted doilies on the polished dark mahogany tables and on the back and arms of their upholstered settee. A grandfather clock ticked in the background. I sipped lemonade while they told me how they would take their own lives in the case of a "mental collapse" or unbearable pain. "No one," said Rachel, "should be kept alive too long if they are suffering. We are well now, but if we choose, we have the *right to die*." Inside the china cabinet was the manual that they obtained from the *Hemlock Society*, an organization that supports suicide (under certain circumstances) and the decriminalization of assistance to a person who has made that decision. Hemlock Society manuals such as *Final Exit* (Humphry, 1991) describe nonviolent methods of committing suicide with prescription barbiturates.

On another day, I found myself in a similar conversation with Harvey (a retired lawyer who looks at least 15 years younger than his 81 years) and his wife, Eileen, a 79-year-old former secretary. Seven years ago, Harvey developed a minor heart ailment. Because they have only one surviving child, who lives in a remote part of Australia, they felt that there was no one to assume responsibility for them should they become ill. They had friends at Franklin Village, so it made sense to add their names to the waiting list. Six years later they moved in.

Harvey and Eileen have living wills.* Their plan is less direct than the one that Rachel and Paul have. Harvey and Eileen have

---

*More than 40 states and the District of Columbia have "Natural Death" legislation that gives patients and their families the right to refuse treatment documented in "living wills." In December 1991, a new federal law went into effect, requiring all federally funded hospitals, nursing homes, and hospices to inform incoming patients of their right to fill out a living will. The federal law was designed to encourage Americans to use this document. Nevertheless, these documents are controversial. For example, a person may be certain about "no heroic means" when he or she is well but may feel differently when death is imminent—and, what is worse, may be unable to communicate that feeling. Also, families who agreed to living wills during the "good times" may be unwilling to allow their loved ones to die without extraordinary interventions during such "bad times." Furthermore, the documents themselves may contain ambiguous language. For example, there are no standardized definitions for "artificial means" or "terminal" or "imminent." Physicians and hospitals, fearing later lawsuits because of such ambiguous wording, may not comply with a living will (Older Women's League, 1986).

no barbiturates in their china cabinet, but they are just as firm in their resolve. In their living wills, they have specified the conditions under which their lives should not be prolonged and have directed family members to refuse treatment and sustenance in their behalf. "We do not want to be kept alive by heroic or extraordinary means," said Eileen. Then she kissed her husband on the cheek and dashed off to teach English to Spanish-speaking mushroom farmers.

At Franklin Village, discussions about death were anything but morose. They ranged from the downright nonchalant to the humorous. One interaction I had with a gentleman I met in the cafeteria is a good example of such "death talk." He said, "I had some extra money a while ago. My stockbroker said he had a good investment for me. The only catch was that it wouldn't bring a dividend for three years. I told him that he was crazy—at my age I don't even buy green bananas!"

Another example of "gallows humor" took place in the same spot several days later. I was sitting at a table having hot dogs and baked beans with two male residents. When I asked them about their aspirations, the relatively *young-old* man said, "I aspire to finish writing the book I started years ago." The second man, who was *old-old* (at least 90) said, "I aspire to finish reading a book."

MAINTAINING HEALTH

Good health is highly valued. Independence or autonomy is impossible without it. Residents spoke of aspirations for staying physically and mentally healthy or improving their current health. The elderly people who spoke about this aspiration all shared the same belief—that is, to stay healthy, one has to be mentally involved and physically active, and the busier the better.

At 103, Jeanette is the oldest resident in the community. She has lived there for 13 years. Hubert and Beth, my resident "research assistants," pointed her out to me on the first day. Beth said, "I will introduce you if you like." But I wasn't ready. Jeanette's mental acuity at age 103 made her somewhat of a celebrity. People referred to her with awe. I was saving her for last, in the same way I never eat the cherry on the top of a sundae until the last bit of ice cream has been licked from the spoon. People would say, "You really must speak with Jeanette," or "Jeanette is remarkable. Make sure you talk to her."

Jeanette is blind, so I was able to observe her without being detected. She was plump for one so old, a handsome woman with wavy white hair. I would see her at meetings (Spiritual Life on Tuesday nights and Current Events on Thursday nights). She was usually sitting up front when I arrived. At other times, I watched her being pushed in her wheelchair on the walkways or in the Center.

One thing puzzled me. Every morning Jeanette (immaculately groomed) would leave her wheelchair at the door of the dining room and enter the room on the arm of a resident or staff member. It seemed as though she was making a "grand entrance." She was certainly regal, but I wondered if she was vain, as well. When I finally called her to request an interview, she said, "Oh, not on Monday. I am going to the hairdresser." We agreed to meet later in the week. Again I thought that appearances seemed to mean a lot to her.

Jeanette was a gracious hostess. Her primary goal, she said, is not to lose her mind. She said that she keeps her mental faculties "by staying in touch with young people" and by studying archeology. Several times a week, resident volunteers read aloud to her. She has just begun a series of books and articles about archeology. Eventually, I asked her why she did not use her wheelchair in the dining room. "Oh, that," she said. "I make sure that although I use the wheelchair most of the time, I walk a half mile a day. My morning walks and my short walks into the dining room three times a day just about does it. I exercise to stay healthy." I also learned that she went to the hairdresser every week because "being old is no excuse for sloppiness." I never again made such assumptions.

SELF-PROTECTION TO MAINTAIN HEALTH

Marianne, an 85-year-old former schoolteacher, lives one floor above Jeanette in the nursing facility. Marianne has already lost her good health. She suffers from osteoporosis and spinal cancer, both of which cause her bones to be extremely brittle. I was startled by her appearance. She is tiny and pale. Her illness has caused her to shrink five inches. It is difficult for her to stand; she is in constant pain.

Marianne is exceedingly frail in body but remarkably robust in spirit. Perhaps she inherited that spirit from her mother, a suffragette. Marianne showed me the crumbling yellowed newspaper clippings that recorded some of her mother's activism.

Despite her pain, Marianne giggles like a schoolgirl. She recalled the day that she entered the dining room after many weeks of illness so severe that she was certain that she would die soon. "When I entered the room," she said, "everyone's face went blank. Then I realized that they all thought that I was dead!" Marianne laughed so hard that for a moment I worried about those frail bones of hers.

Even though Marianne has no illusions about regaining her health, she wishes to protect what little reserve she has. One day, another resident of the nursing facility—a woman who spends most of her days calling for her mother—was wandering in the hall, disoriented and agitated. Marianne approached the woman and asked, "Can you help me with my zipper?" The woman became lucid and with her good arm (she had had a stroke) she lifted the zipper of Marianne's dress. Then Marianne helped her back to her room.

Later, Marianne related this experience to her son. He became distressed, pointing out that the woman, in her agitation, could have used her good arm to strike Marianne. Marianne acknowledged, "My bones are so brittle that another fall would be traumatic. I need to stop doing what comes naturally and protect myself."

STAYING BUSY, STAYING HEALTHY

Living in a continuing-care retirement community helps, but it
does not guarantee autonomy. It is merely an environment in
which independence can be prolonged. As long as residents
maintain physical health, they can maintain some level of autonomy at Franklin Village. The greatest threat to their autonomy
is going "stir crazy."

Alton, a 79-year-old retired engineer, is typical of the busy
people at Franklin Village. He has a myriad of hobbies and activities that consume his day and, he believes, keep him from going
stir crazy (losing his senses) like some of the unfortunate residents in the nursing-care unit.

Hubert introduced me to Alton in the busiest place in the
community—the wood shop. Alton was bent over a machine
that was stamping out small white letters on little green plastic
signs. Hubert had to tap him on the shoulder several times to get
his attention. Alton didn't seem pleased to interrupt his work,
and he was not at all interested in me or my study.

I didn't want to intrude where I wasn't welcome, but at the
same time I thought, "What kind of researcher am I if I give up
so easily?" I remembered the green plastic tag that was pinned
to my blouse and said, "You must be the one who made this."
"That's right," he said proudly, "I make all the signs and name
tags here."

In the 14 years that Alton has lived in Franklin Village, he has
made thousands of signs and tags. "And every one was perfect.
Nothing leaves the shop that is not perfect. Why, I had to make
yours at least four times until it looked right. Why in the world
did they want your name so large?" he asked.

Alton is also involved in the Armchair Traveler Club. Members take turns presenting travel slides to the group. Alton,
always the perfectionist, is the leader. He insists that the presen-
tations are scripted into stories that are entertaining. "It upsets
me, when someone simply says, 'This is a _____' or 'This

town is called _____,'" he says. Alton doesn't mind writing all the scripts and helping other members put their slides into sequence.

He loves to be in charge and to arrange and direct things. When they were young, Alton and his wife participated in community theater. When their children were small, they took turns staying home. When his wife was in a play, he baby-sat. In the next play, he would act or direct, and she would mind the kids. Eventually, when the children were grown, they performed together. Always a busy person, Alton is convinced that he must maintain his "busyness" in order to retain his mental faculties.

The same can be said for Grover, an 80-year-old retired pediatrician. Grover's hobby keeps both himself and Alton busy. Two years ago, when Grover moved into the community, he noticed the many beautiful trees on the grounds. (There are more than 600.) Always interested in horticulture, but never having enough time to pursue it, he had an idea that would keep his mind and his body active. He got permission from Franklin Village to label every tree on the campus with its Latin and English names. Alton made the plastic signs and Grover hung them up. Grover's wife says, "Taking a walk with Grover is like taking a walk with a dog. He has to stop at every tree."

Grover, Alton, and even 103-year-old Jeanette seem to know intuitively what some medical researchers are "discovering"— that is, that "the body, to an increasing degree, is now felt to 'rust out' rather than 'wear out' ... exercising an organ presents a strategy for modifying the aging process" (Fries, 1980, p. 133).

No longer are we satisfied with longevity. It is important that extra years be healthy years. The term *life expectancy* has less relevance than it once had. Living a long life is a goal that medical science, nutrition, and improved health practices have placed within reach of most older people. There has been a remarkable increase in life expectancy since the turn of the century (see Table 3.1). Fewer people die prematurely in childhood or while giving birth. Acute illnesses, mainly infectious diseases like tuberculosis, rheumatic fever, smallpox, and polio, have ceased to be the threats they once were. (The AIDS epidemic is a recent exception.)

TABLE 3.1
Life Expectancy at Birth and Age 65 by Sex: 1900–1985
(with 1988 Data Added)

Year	Both Sexes	All Races Male	Female
At Birth:			
1900[a,b]	47.3	46.3	48.3
1950[b]	68.2	65.6	71.1
1960[b]	69.7	66.6	73.1
1970	70.9	67.1	74.8
1980	73.7	70.0	77.4
1985[b,c]	74.7	71.2	78.2
1988-s2d	74.9	—	—
At Age 65:			
1900–02[a,b]	11.9	11.5	12.2
1950[b]	13.9	12.8	15.0
1960[b]	14.3	12.8	15.8
1970	15.2	13.1	17.0
1980	16.4	14.1	18.3
1985[b,c]	16.8	14.6	18.6

Source: National Center for Health Statistics, *Health, United States, 1986.* DHHS Pub. No. (PHS)87-1232. Washington: Department of Health and Human Services, December 1986.

[a] Ten states and the District of Columbia.
[b] Includes deaths of nonresidents of the United States.
[c] Provisional data.
[d] Data added from National Center for Health Statistics.

Some scientists speculate that we are close to achieving the maximum life span of our species (Fries, 1980). Unfortunately, the later years are often fraught with symptoms of chronic illnesses that are typically associated with aging—heart disease, coronary-artery disease, stroke, diabetes, hypertension, chronic lung disease, cancer, dementia. Chronic illnesses may impede functioning to such an extent that even though an individual lives to an old age, the quality of his or her life holds little to envy.

What Grover and others like him are seeking is what gerontologists call *compression of morbidity* (Fries, 1980). Simply put, this means that the onset of chronic diseases is postponed so that *morbidity* (the period of time one suffers from chronic debilitating diseases) is *compressed* or shortened. In other words, people live long, vigorous lives, and they are ill for only a brief period prior to their deaths. Residents of Franklin Village would call this a "good death."

BUSYWORK

During the first few weeks at Franklin Village, I was impressed by the residents' vitality. Posted on bulletin boards were notices of numerous activities such as committee meetings, trips, and lectures. I met new people every day and heard glorious aspirations about learning, traveling, improving oneself, and serving others. I was comforted by the vitality and forward-looking perspective I witnessed. It was heartening to see aging in such a positive light. And then I met Elsie.

Elsie had been an internationally known scientist. She would not tell me her age. She would only say that she was over 65. Dr. Thomas had warned me about her before we met. Elsie was "difficult." Elsie was a member of the Institutional Review Board, one of the groups that had earlier judged and eventually approved of my study at Franklin Village.

During the period of review, Elsie sent me a note expressing reservations about my study and criticizing my proposal. She objected vehemently to my residence in the community and saw my methodology as "impossible" and "undisciplined." Fortunately, for my sake, she was out of town when the board took its final vote. (Remember, this was a Quaker group that made decisions by consensus.)

I was intimidated by Elsie. Not only was she very famous, but it was clear that she didn't think too much of me. Nevertheless, I was intrigued by something she wrote, and I wanted to talk to her about it. Elsie had written, "One must not confuse aspirations with busywork."

Elsie was cordial when I visited her in her apartment. She showed me the books she had written; she described her laboratories and experiments and lectures. She told me about her travels across the continent and throughout the world. I noted that Elsie acted as though she were still involved in all this activity, although most of it had occurred nearly forty years before.

Finally, Elsie asked about my work. I began by extolling the virtues of the wood shop and ceramic studio, admiring the products of those activities and what I understood as "aspirations in action." Elsie said, "Don't overestimate what goes on there. Much of that is mere busywork, not aspiration."

She differentiated aspirations and busywork along the lines of most dictionaries—that is, busywork is designed to "take up time," not necessarily to yield productions, whereas aspirations (and activities involved in them) are designed to fulfill the strong desire for achievement. She said, "When one has an aspiration, the goal is very important. When one is engaged in busywork, the goal is of little importance. What is important is keeping busy."

My conversations with Elsie illuminated my understanding of what I experienced at Franklin Village. From that point on, I explored the meaning of activities. Most of the time, they were goal-directed. Sometimes what initially appeared to be merely busywork (e.g., pinning signs on trees) was the means to achieve the goal of maintaining mental and physical health. However, I discovered that busywork did exist. Usually, it was a way of coping with feelings of depression or the pain of what one resident called "the rhythm of death in a retirement community."

Beth, my unofficial research assistant and friend, helped me to understand this "underside" of life in the community. Beth was extremely active. Yet she agreed with Elsie and talked about her own feelings of depression. "Lots of older folks are depressed, even here. People don't talk about it much," she said. "After all, you don't see the ones who are alone in their apartments in bed. Everyone here will die. That's the disadvantage of a place like this. It is very hard to lose friends so consistently. It is difficult to see friends, who were formerly vital and brilliant, fail. It is frustrating to see friends who do not accept their limitations and make the necessary accommodations. They refuse to wear hearing aids or insist upon retaining their apartments when they clearly need supervised care. Not every busy person is a person happily fulfilling their aspirations. Elsie is right. You have to check carefully."

In the early days of the new field of *gerontology*, there was quite a brouhaha about whether or not *level of activity* indicated *successful aging*. The proponents of *activity theory* (Havighurst & Albrecht, 1953) proposed that the continuation or increase in involvement with family and friends, participation in voluntary organizations and social groups, and the pursuit of hobbies and interests correlate highly with measures of life satisfaction. Hence, successful aging was characterized by lots of activity. On the other hand, proponents of *disengagement theory* (Cumming & Henry, 1961) noted that the older person and society tended to distance from one another (the old person may cut down on activities while society forces retirement and encourages age segregation). Subjects who were thus disengaged correlated highly with measures of high morale.*

Activity, as Elsie and Beth helped me to understand, could mean many things. It could represent vigorous older people fully enjoying themselves in the pursuit of their aspirations, dreams, and goals for the future, or it could serve as a way to keep healthy or a means to ward off feelings of sadness and pain related to loss. I suspect that it could also represent lifelong patterns that are hard to change—for instance, a strong work ethic.

Ekerdt (1986) calls the emphasis people place on keeping busy

---

*In gerontological research, the term "morale" is often used interchangeably with the term "life satisfaction." Cumming and Henry (1961) do not define it other than to say: "Because people know what is meant when they hear one another say, 'My morale is low,' and because a number of works have used this term, we use it throughout this chapter. It is meant to have its ordinary connotation" (p. 129). Lawton (1977), originator of a widely used morale measure, defined high morale as a "basic sense of satisfaction with oneself—a feeling that there is a place in the environment for oneself—that people and things in one's life offer some satisfaction to the individual—a fit between personal needs and what the environment offers . . . [and] a certain acceptance of what cannot be changed" (p. 148).

during retirement the "busy ethic" (p. 239). For people who identify work with virtue and see it as justifying their existence,
busyness provides a moral continuity between working and
retirement (thus legitimizing retirement). It defends retired people against judgments of obsolescence, gives definition to the
retirement role, and helps retirement to "fit" the prevailing soci-
etal norms.

The busy ethic, however, does not apply to all retirees. It tends
to be a value of the *young-old*—those who are not burdened with
chronic illness and frailty (Ekerdt, 1986). Also, there are some
retirees who are relatively young and healthy but choose to use
that vigor in the pursuit of pleasure rather than busyness. This
will be addressed in Chapter 7. But first, Chapter 4 will explore
the value of personal growth.

CHAPTER 4

PERSONAL GROWTH

"To become better than before"

SPIRITUALITY

Every afternoon at a quarter past twelve, Hope can be seen speeding over the rise on a motorized buggy (on her way to the noontime meal at the Center), her white hair flying in the breeze. Fifteen years ago, at 70, she insisted on taking the apartment that was the farthest from the Center and which required a climb up a small hill.

"The walk was good for me," she explains. "When I was a young country doc, I was used to house calls in the hills." Unfortunately, at 75, Hope was stricken with pernicious anemia, which made the daily walk virtually impossible.

Hope's apartment is frayed at the edges. The upholstery has places where the pattern has worn off. In some spots, white stuffing peers through the blue threads. The living room is neat, clean, and—above all—practical. Hope's chair is in front of the large window (where she can watch the birds feed) and near the phone (so she doesn't have to get up to answer it). Her books are within arm's reach.

Hope initiated many of the committees at Franklin Village. More recently, she has withdrawn from an active role to a more contemplative one. "This," she says, "is natural and good. As people age, there is a diminishment in the physical field and a growth of the spirit. I am happy to focus on different things now." She "works" on her spiritual side by reading spiritual material and by meditating.

"Isn't it hard," I asked, "to give up all the activities you used to have?" "It's not hard, because it is more difficult to continue them than to give them up," she answered.

Four or five times a week, visually impaired residents come to Hope's apartment to listen to her read aloud. Sometimes they choose the reading material. More often, she chooses it. She likes to alternate between spiritual and religious topics and light humor. During one of my visits, Jeanette, the 103-year-old blind woman, called to ask when Hope would be well enough to read to her again. Hope's knees were more painful than usual, so she had cancelled that week's reading hour.

I liked Hope immediately, but despite that—or perhaps because of it—I told her a lie. We were discussing the way in which the world had changed during her lifetime when she asked, "You are not divorced, are you?" Separated four weeks from my husband, I lied, "Oh, no, I am happily married." To that, she replied, "I'm glad. No one stays married anymore."

My lie was "automatic." Later I realized it came from my assumption that an old person could not possibly understand divorce or think positively about someone who left a spouse after 25 years. I quickly changed the subject. I was uneasy about the lie, which robbed me of the opportunity to explore her views on marriage and family.

One month later, I confessed. Hope understood. "Don't worry. It is perfectly all right. I'm an old country doctor; I don't disapprove of anything. Nothing more needs to be said, unless you want to talk about it."

At first I said, "No, I don't need to talk about it." Eventually I did tell her my story. Hope was compassionate, accepting, and wise. "After all," she said, "in the old days, people married and promised to be together for the rest of their days. It was a simpler matter then because the rest of their lives might not be more than twenty years. Now it is quite different. People live for a very long time. Marriages could last for fifty years, even. That's quite another matter, isn't it?"

She continued, "In life, you have many disappointments and much sadness. But each one of those things has something to teach you. Martin Buber [the Hasidic philosopher] said that in this world each person is exactly where he or she should be."

Annabelle (an 86-year-old former schoolteacher) would probably agree. I met with Annabelle for only a half hour in her room in the nursing facility, and yet I felt that I knew her better than many of my friends and family members.

This "knowing" was achieved without ever finding out about her life before Franklin Village or what her life had been like in the 15 years she had lived in the community. The only thing I know about is a recent trauma she experienced, which I will report here exactly as she told it to me.

One month before we met, Annabelle had become incapacitated with a heart ailment that necessitated the much-dreaded move from an independent apartment to a room in the nursing-care facility. The relocation threw her into an "emotional tailspin." Annabelle explained, "I thought that my left brain was getting confused with my right brain. Things around me seemed to change and melt into each other so quickly, I could hardly keep anything straight."

She believes that the trauma of learning about her heart condition and losing her independent life-style triggered the mental decline. The most terrible part was that she did not know if she would recover. She feared that she would have to live the remainder of her days in a confused state. When I met her, she was much improved but was still not her former self. She would like to know if her experience was the result of the physical trauma or an emotional reaction, or both, although she does not expect to find the answers.

As a young woman, Annabelle became interested in parapsychology. She read about St. Anthony's spiritual growth and mystical experiences. She wondered, "Was this what happened to me?" Now, emerging from the experience, she has noticed a difference in herself. Annabelle is convinced that while in the experience, she learned all she ever needs to know. Now, when she participates in discussion groups, she knows all the answers. Despite this, she keeps the revelations to herself so that others may "find enlightenment at their own pace."

Her goal is to "touch lives in a way that is comforting and supportive." When I asked her how she would do this, Annabelle said, "Just be." Most people are too busy evaluating, judging, and analyzing. Life should be effortless. When you are just being, you do not get caught in the duality of either/or. If the phone rings, I don't have to concern myself with 'Who is it?' or 'Should I answer it?' It could be terrible news, but on the other hand, it could be something important. If you are just being, you effortlessly just 'do.' Whatever you do is absolutely right." Hope said essentially the same thing when she said, "Each person is exactly where he or she should be."

In Annabelle's view, people are born with different capabilities. She said, "Some [spiritually] grow rapidly, and some grow more slowly. Bitter people simply are not growing. They have obstacles that they have to work out for themselves before they can grow again. Sometimes, one word from another person can be the right word to help them overcome the obstacle. At other times, no one has the right word, and the person must find their own way." She was interrupted by a nurse who came in to give her a bath.

As I left her room, Annabelle said, "I'm glad you came. It was good for me because I have not said these things to anyone yet. You are like an analyst." I said, "I don't feel like an analyst; I feel like a student." Annabelle smiled and said, "That's the best kind of person to be." We looked at each other and shared a very nice moment before I departed.

The Spiritual Life Committee meets every Tuesday evening in one of the rooms in the Center's lower level. Hope explained that the committee chooses a book and discusses it for several weeks. The group's purpose is to gain a fuller understanding of religion, spirituality, and parapsychology. The meeting is informal—no structure, no leader, and no goals other than to understand and enhance spiritual well-being among those residents who care to participate.

Malcolm, a 78-year-old retired social worker, invited me to the Spiritual Life Committee meeting. The assignment for that week was *The New Religions* (Needleman, 1987). I borrowed his dog-eared copy.

Malcolm regards retirement as his third career. His first was his formal schooling; his second was his work career. One of his goals for his third career is to resolve (in his own mind) the apparent dichotomy between religion and science. Malcolm relishes his freedom to pursue answers to this spiritual dilemma.

As an avid reader, he seeks out illuminating readings. He collects quotations, passages, and sections of works that uplift him and aid him in his spiritual quest. Someday, his family, especially the grandchildren, will enjoy the fruits of his labors. Malcolm plans to compile the material into an anthology to share with his loved ones.

Among the residents I met at the Spiritual Life Committee meeting was Lynnette. At 92, Lynnette still works, albeit part-time. She is a concert pianist and music teacher. Whenever I think about "aging gracefully," I think of Lynnette with her delicate bone structure and fair complexion. Unlike most residents, her skin is not marked with brown "age spots." Her hair frames her face in a silvery white bouffant. Lynnette's clothing is modest (high necklines, long sleeves) and tastefully coordinated on an uncommonly erect frame.

Several times during the discussion that evening, people turned to her and asked, "Well, what do you think, Lynnette?" Later, Lynnette explained, "People tend to defer to me on spiritual matters because they know that all my life I have been a 'spiritual worker.' My lifelong aspiration is to make the unconscious conscious. I haven't succeeded, but I continue the effort." She has meditated for 30 years.

My friends Hubert and Beth also mentioned spirituality in their lives. Hubert, always the popular and gregarious resident, occasionally seeks seclusion. "Solitude," he says, "is the means by which I receive 'refueling' for my spiritual journey." Beth enhances her spiritual side via a bright orange wig and cherry-red nose. As I mentioned earlier, she is one of two women who don clown costumes and face-paint to entertain sick and dying residents. "Clowning," she explains, "helps me to become a 'whole person.'" She learned her technique from a "clowning" clergyman.

Annabelle, Hope, Malcolm, Lynnette, and other residents value spiritual growth. Each one understands spirituality in his or her own way, and each quest is different. Like so many other important constructs, *spiritual well-being* is nearly impossible to *operationalize*. A widely used definition comes from the National Interfaith Coalition on Aging (1975): "Spiritual well-being is the affirmation of life in a relationship with God, self, community, and environment that nurtures and celebrates wholeness" (p. 280).

Ellison (1983) goes beyond the concept of spiritual well-being to explore the concept of *spirituality*. He writes that the human spirit "enables and motivates us to search for meaning and purpose in life, to seek the supernatural or some meaning which transcends us, to wonder about our origins and our identities, to require morality and equity" (p. 331).

Late life seems uniquely suited for this endeavor. It is usually a time when there is a "turning inward." Levinson (1978) describes this turning inward in the following way:

> [It] does not mean that a man becomes more selfish or vain. Just the opposite. It means that he becomes less interested in obtaining the rewards offered by society and more interested in utilizing his own inner resources. The voices within the self become, as it were, more audible and more worthy of his attention. He continues to be actively engaged with the voices and realities of the external world, but he seeks a new balance in which the self has greater primacy. (p. 36)

LEARNING

Hubert's advice about aging well is, "Don't fossilize; keep growing." Many residents talked about what they still wanted to learn and experience. Many of our conversations rekindled their memories of the influence of teachers, mentors, and parents— memories they were eager to share.

Two incidents in Malcolm's childhood influenced his entire life. The first occurred when he was in his first semester at a strict religious boarding school. At exam time, Malcolm was feeling "puny and fatigued." A Brother who was a strict taskmaster but who was also kind to him gave him a "pep talk." He said that in spite of one's puniness, fatigue, and despair, one should "end strong." Malcolm never forgot that simple command.

The second incident took place when he was walking downtown with his grandfather, an attorney. They passed a man who was lying on the ground in an alleyway. His grandfather greeted the man, who looked up from the pavement and returned the greeting. Young Malcolm was perplexed and asked his grandfather who the man was. His grandfather said that the man was an attorney who had "let the drink get to him." Then he turned to Malcolm, shook his finger, and said, "Malcolm, never let yourself go."

The importance of these two events was not limited to their content. Malcolm feels that he was open and "vulnerable" to the lessons contained in these childhood experiences. "Once I recognized that," he said, "I aspired to always be open and receptive to learning."

I looked forward to meeting another resident, Simon. Hubert and Beth told me that the 97-year-old retired chest surgeon was "special," someone "not to miss." Our initial contact was characteristic of his straightforward, unassuming manner, although it did startle me. I telephoned Simon, explaining the purpose of my study and asking if I could visit him in his apartment on Monday at 10 a.m. Simon responded, "Monday at 10 a.m. is fine, but don't be upset if I'm not here when you arrive. I often become confused and wander about. I'm 97 years old, you know." Simon was, in fact, in his apartment when I arrived, and he was fully in command of his faculties.

Simon told me, "My aspirations have much to do with my curiosity. I have never had a bored moment in my life." Like Malcolm, Simon heard something in his childhood that influenced his entire life. As a youngster, Simon was a poor student. He preferred to read Sherlock Holmes books rather than apply himself to his studies. He was constantly in trouble because he was never prepared for class. He says that it was worth the trouble. He had a great time reading those books and doing what he pleased.

Eventually, Simon devised a technique to avoid trouble. "I would ask the teacher question after question," he explained, "so that the teacher would not have enough time to ask me questions." He was doing that one day, when finally his teacher said, "Simon, never let anyone take away that divine curiosity you have." Ironically, this statement changed his life. His questions had been, of course, merely a stalling tactic and not necessarily a demonstration of curiosity. Nevertheless, he thought about the teacher's statement, and he began to let his curiosity take free rein. Soon, he started to set goals and concentrate.

Not long after this incident, he met a surgeon. Simon was so impressed with the man that he decided that he also wanted to be a surgeon. He applied his curiosity to anything medical and, without help, set out to accomplish what he needed to do to get into medical school.

Simon continues to be curious and receptive to learning. He said, "I am especially lucky with books. Whenever I read a book, it turns out to be a book that I need at that time—that is, I always come across a message or theme that I need or that enlightens me." Three years ago, when he was 94, Simon went on a three-week tour of China. He prepared himself by reading everything he could about the country. He was accompanied on the trip by his son—also an elderly man.

Aspirations to learn included desires for fuller understanding.

Lynnette wanted to understand music the way Beethoven did, although she doubted that she ever would. Some talked of wanting to "keep up" in their understanding of the rapidly changing world. Others expressed aspirations to master bodies of knowledge (e.g., learn a language, or learn the Latin names for the trees in the community) or develop skills (e.g., managing finances or becoming computer literate).

Martha, a 91-year-old weaver, is one of the residents who continues to aspire to learn. She told me, with much pride, that "I *never* bought anything I could make myself." This practice has nothing to do with limited funds or inaccessibility of goods, but rather it has to do with her love of a challenge. She is the only woman to have ever worked alongside the men in the wood shop.

During the 15 years she has lived at Franklin Village, she has built three dollhouses. The first was a log cabin. She spent countless hours researching in the library so that she could accurately recreate a log cabin. A second dollhouse was a miniature-scaled replica of a church she attended in her youth. She made the trip back to her hometown to study its dimensions and details, including the stained glass windows. The third was the house of her childhood, recreated from memory. Martha did the electrical wiring, wove the bedspreads and curtains, and built all the furniture. "If I don't know how to do something, I get a book on it and simply learn how," she says.

Martha and I chatted in the weaving room, while she wove a white and gray shawl with gold threads. She explained that the threads were of uneven strength and quality, making the cloth beautiful but extremely difficult to weave. The technique required her to tie hundreds of tiny knots. At 91, Martha and others value learning and apparently are still capable of learning.

INTELLIGENCE AND WISDOM

Researchers in intelligence agree that older people can function well intellectually and can continue to learn, despite the significant declines in intellectual performance that may begin for some adults in their early or middle fifties (Schaie, 1983).

There is a dual nature to intellectual functioning that is particularly useful in understanding the inner experience of the elderly. This *dual-process framework of intelligence* (Baltes, Smith, Staudinger, & Sowarka, 1990) is an extension of the original conceptual framework of the famous Cattell-Horn theory of fluid-crystallized intelligence (Cattell, 1971; Horn, 1970).

Fluid intelligence (mechanics) refers to the mechanics of intelligence, such as the speed of information-processing and memory. *Crystallized intelligence* (pragmatics) refers to both the facts one knows and the strategies or application of that knowledge. Both types of intelligence increase during childhood and adolescence. Fluid intelligence, however, shows a turning point in early adulthood and then drops. Crystallized intelligence, on the other hand, continues to increase, but at a slower rate after early adulthood (see Figure 4.1) (Staudinger, Cornelius, & Baltes, 1989).

The computer can be used as a metaphor to explain the difference in intellectual functioning in early and late life. We can think of cognition as consisting of three parts—hardware, software, and data. The computer hardware (the processing chip, all the wires, and other electronic and mechanical components) represent the brain and central nervous system, which drive fluid intelligence. The computer software (programs that control the computer) stand for a person's styles and strategies of cognition and behavior (i.e., crystallized intelligence). The data base of information stored inside the computer is an individual's lifetime of accumulated knowledge.

In an older person, the "hardware" may become worn out, less reliable, and not quite "state of the art." Nevertheless, the person might possess a strong body of data and especially powerful "software" in the form of strategies of thinking.

In contrast, a young person, with a faster processing "chip," is less likely to have as much accumulated data or the software to make efficient use of the hardware. Unless the hardware suffers

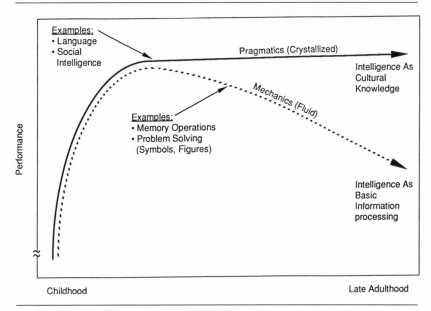

Figure 4-1. Multidimensionality and multidirectionality of life-span intelligence. (From: "The Aging of Intelligence: Potential and Limits" by U.M. Staudinger, S.W. Cornelius, & P.B. Baltes, 1989, in *Annuals of the America Academy of Political and Social Science*, Vol. 503, p. 47. Copyright © 1989 by Sage Publications, Inc. Reprinted by permission.)

some serious defect (as in Alzheimer's patients), the somewhat slower system may not be a limiting factor for tasks. In fact, the "wisdom" of the older person's "system" (the strong software and extensive body of data) may prove superior to the sleeker, faster, but less "wise" younger system (Perlmutter, 1988).

It has been established that, with training, older adults can improve their performance on tasks in the domain of fluid intelligence. The gains that can be made in those tasks are roughly comparable to the declines that occur between the ages of 60 and 80 (Staudinger, Cornelius, & Baltes, 1989),

The most encouraging finding is that stability and growth in crystallized/pragmatic intelligence can offset or compensate for the declines in fluid/mechanic intelligence, which means that an older person may maintain performance or even excel at something. One study showed that "tapping speed," a component skill involved in typing, was significantly slower in older typists than in younger typists. Surprisingly, though, no age differences were found between the younger and older adults' typing performance. The likely explanation is that the older typists compensated for the decline in tapping speed by reading farther ahead in the text to be typed (Salthouse, 1984). Since tapping speed is considered an indicator of cognitive mechanics and reading text an indicator of knowledge-based pragmatics, it appears that the older subjects simply overcame their deficits by developing a strategy based on procedural knowledge (Staudinger, Cornelius, & Baltes, 1989).

Besides compensation, another determinant of whether or not healthy older people continue to function well intellectually is whether they *believe* they can and whether they can adjust their efforts to match a realistic assessment of their limits and potential.

In Chapter 3, I discussed "compression of morbidity" (Fries, 1980), which represents the goal of reducing the period of illness in old age to a brief period before death. *Compression of cognitive dysfunction* (Staudinger, Cornelius, & Baltes, 1989) is a similar concept that represents the goal of maintaining intellectual functioning to the very last stage of life.

An older person might not only maintain functioning, but might also be capable of becoming an expert in the "fundamental pragmatics of life,"* the domain associated with wisdom. The attainment of wisdom may be an aspect of intellectual functioning in which elderly people have an opportunity to hold "world records." This makes sense when we consider the stability and growth of crystallized intelligence through the life span and the

---

*The "fundamental pragmatics of life" refers to "a system of knowledge about the variations and conditions of human development across the life course, human nature and conduct, life tasks and goals, social relationships, and the dynamics of intergenerational relations. ... This domain encompasses various kinds of abilities: for example, to integrate contradictory evidence, to deal with uncertainty, to simplify complexity without becoming too restrictive in one's considerations, and to revise earlier decisions and admit mistakes" (Staudinger, Cornelius, & Baltes, 1989, pp. 54–55).

opportunity that older people have had to accumulate expert factual knowledge about the human condition.

EGO IDEAL

In the corridor, halfway between the nursing-care wing of the Center and the main dining room, is a very unusual couch. It is not exactly ugly, but one could hardly call it beautiful. Large brilliant pink and orange poppies intermingle with green parrots on a sky-blue background of tufted velvet. Were it not for the garish covering, the couch's high curved legs and graceful back would make it an elegant piece of furniture.

Most mornings, at 9 a.m. and again at 11 a.m., one can find 87-year-old Suzanne resting on the couch on her way to and from breakfast in the dining room. The settee once belonged to her. When she moved into Franklin Village, Suzanne could not bear to give the couch away, and it was too large to fit into her apartment. Fortunately, the management proposed that if she had its worn upholstery recovered, they would place it in the Center. She agreed.

Eventually, when Suzanne "came under the roof," she realized that the beloved sofa provided a "halfway" resting place that allowed her to "go out" for breakfast rather than have it brought to her room like the other nursing-care residents. From her colorful sofa, Suzanne observed the busy activities of the Center. That is where I met her.

Suzanne is the kind of person you either love or avoid. Some of the residents are "put off" by her appearance and manner. She has only one brown front tooth on her lower jaw. Her hair is usually uncombed, and she wears the same set of spotted clothes (a mauve pants-suit with a pink T-shirt) every day. She has a reputation for speaking her mind—and not always graciously.

She usually sits alone on the couch or at the same corner table in the dining room. She explains, "I *choose* to be by myself because my asthma would annoy any date." Suzanne and I shared many meals, and I never heard her cough or wheeze.

One day, I escorted her from the couch to her room. "You can come in," she said, "but I'm not a good housekeeper, never was. Don't care about that sort of thing very much." Papers, magazines, and cardboard boxes were strewn all over the floor. There was some half-eaten food on the table, and there was a strange odor in the room. Suzanne kept her beloved books in the "library," which turned out to be her bathroom.

"In this box are my haiku. Do you know what a haiku is?" she asked. "They are short little Japanese poems that must have a certain structure. I am not very disciplined, you know, but I have written a haiku every day for the last 50 years. I do it for discipline. Soon, I shall write a haiku for you."

Suzanne went on, "All my life I've been too pert. My only aspiration is to stay out of trouble. I never seem to be able to do that," she said with a smile. In the next instant, I had an example. A housekeeper arrived. Suzanne used my visit as an opportunity to avoid this weekly intrusion. "I can't possibly have my room cleaned while I am entertaining a visitor," she told the cleaning woman, who then obediently went away.

The next day, when we sat on the couch, Suzanne said, "The nursing staff is very unhappy with me. They told me that cleaning is very important and that sending away the cleaning person is improper. But," she continued pertly, "I told them that yes, I know how important it is to clean. When I am dead, just kick over my body and sweep around it!"

Nevertheless, Suzanne would frequently make great efforts to conform to the behavior of other residents. She even "picked up" someone to help her. To "pick up" someone at Franklin Village simply means to befriend him or her. In this case, she picked up a young groundkeeper, Tim, who cheerfully tries to help her organize her belongings. This is no easy task because the work is slowed down with her stories about each piece of memorabilia. More often than not, the item stays exactly where it is, but Tim and Suzanne have a delightful afternoon.

One day at breakfast she lamented, "I wish that I was a 'lovely lady.'" "What is a lovely lady?" I asked. Suzanne smiled at me with that mischievous smile I had come to know and said, "A lovely lady would not tell this story." Suzanne then told the following joke:

Once, a researcher, just like you, came to the old folks' home [Suzanne refuses to call it a retirement community]. The researcher was studying sexuality in the aged. The researcher asked an old man if he was still having intercourse. The old man replied, "Why, yes." The researcher said, "And how often do you have it?" The old man said, "Once a year." The researcher replied, "Oh, well, I am sorry to hear that, but you look so happy." To that, the old man said, "Well, yes—tonight's the night!"

Suzanne's laugh was definitely not ladylike.

Later that same day, Suzanne presented me with a haiku written in a "ladylike" hand, especially for me:

> Blue-grey rolling clouds
> Little path way wanders off
> Young friend smiles—gives hand.

Noreen, 77 years old, says, "I don't mind becoming a character, but I do mind my tendency to criticize." Bernadette, at 78, says, "I wish that I could become as bright as most of the residents of Franklin Village."

Even Jeanette, limited by age and blindness, wishes to be "more of a blessing to others." Ida, 85, says that she would like to have more courage. Should her husband die, she will look to other women—that is, other widows—in the community who have been able to make the adjustment from married life to single life. She aspires to pattern herself after these "successful" widows.

"Acceptance" (to become more accepting of others or to be

more accepting of oneself) is another common goal. Beth gets frustrated with residents who deny their obvious limitations. She tires of having to shout at friends who refuse to use hearing aids. It troubles her to witness the hardships of other residents who also refuse devices that would assist them.

Beth says, "*When*, not *if*, I become debilitated, I hope that I will accept the inevitable. It's easy to say all this when I am in pretty good shape, but I know that I could be like that too. I wish I was more patient with the people who have trouble accepting their losses."

The aspiration to "become better than before" is not uncommon at Franklin Village. These wishes are based on an idealized image of the self that Freud called the *ego ideal* (see, e.g., Eidelberg, 1973). More women than men expressed such longings. One wonders if this indicates a gender difference—that is, that older women are more likely than older men to experience dissatisfaction with themselves. Perhaps it means that older women are merely more willing to admit their deficits. In any case, the majority of the people who expressed such wishes, unlike most residents, were nonprofessionals, unskilled workers, and homemakers.

Those social scientists who support the notion of personal growth throughout the life span usually express that growth in terms of *stage theory*. Stages are discrete periods, although their onset and duration vary between individuals. They may or may not be age-related. Each stage provides a central task to achieve or a dilemma to resolve. Individuals may be propelled into subsequent stages by biological maturation, social pressures, or role demands (e.g., school), regardless of how they fared in previous stages. Other theories propose that individuals may be "stuck" in one stage, not progressing to the next hierarchical plane until they successfully achieve the current developmental or life task(s).

It was not until the writings of Erik Erikson (1963) that social scientists began to accept that personal growth continues into adulthood and old age. Erikson's *stages of psychosocial development*

(Table 4.1) is predicated on the notion that the sense of *identity* emerges gradually throughout life and that each stage has the potential for a continuum of outcomes (from the optimum to the less healthy—e.g., trust vs. mistrust). Erikson addressed the later years in Stage 8, ego integrity vs. despair. However, that last stage covers a broad period (50 and over) and is rather nonspecific.

Peck (1968) felt that Erikson's model was more of a representation of the resolutions of the previous stages than a clear depiction of the major dilemmas of the later years. He expanded Erikson's schema in his *stages in psychological development in the second half of life* (Table 4.2), dividing the periods into two chronological divisions, *middle age* and *old age*. Within these two periods, stages may occur in an individually determined sequence.

In a third model, Loevinger's (1976) *stages of ego development* (Table 4.3), the stages are also only loosely connected to age. Movement from one stage to the next is accomplished only when the individual has completed the development in the previous stage. This is quite different from Erikson's model, in which one moves on to the next stage despite an unsatisfactory resolution of the previous stage.

These three models constitute a useful framework with which to consider the residents' values and their aspirations toward spirituality, learning, and ego ideal. Although these aspirations are not exclusive to the elderly, they can be understood as characteristic of the later stages of life according to the models of Erikson, Peck, and Loevinger.

For example, Hope certainly seems to have traversed Peck's stages of psychological development in old age. She went from being a physically active country doctor to being an active community organizer at Franklin Village. Now, in the last stages of her life, and in great pain, she has transcended former vocations and physical pain to quietly focus on spiritual self-fulfillment and to helping blind neighbors gain what they seek from the written word. Her later years are free of regrets or bitterness.

I was the recipient of her wisdom (during a crisis in my life) when she suggested that I was "exactly" where I should be and

TABLE 4.1
Erikson's Stages of Psychosocial Development*

Stage	Description
1. Basic Trust vs. Mistrust (0-1 yr.)	Babies must form loving, trusting relationships with caregivers or risk developing a pervasive sense of mistrust of others, of themselves, and of their ability to cope with inner desires and external demands.
2. Autonomy vs. Shame and Doubt (2-3 yrs.)	Energy is directed toward skill development. Children learn control, but risk developing a sense of shame if parents overcontrol them.
3. Initiative vs. Guilt (4-5 yrs.)	Children continue to become more assertive and take initiative, but risk excessive guilt from their newly emerged consciences.
4. Industry vs. Inferiority (6-12 yrs.)	School-age children dealing with the demands of learning may be proud of their new skills, while being at risk for developing feelings of inferiority.
5. Identity vs. Role Confusion (13-18 yrs.)	Individuals struggle to achieve a sense of identity (i.e., a consistent notion of their own beliefs, values, and goals). Failure results in confusion and perhaps emotional crisis.
6. Intimacy vs. Isolation (19-25 yrs.)	Young adults must risk becoming fused with another to create an intimate relationship or suffer feelings of loneliness and isolation.
7. Generativity vs. Stagnation (26-50 yrs.)	Adults must immerse themselves in guiding and nurturing younger generations. If an adult does not have the opportunity to enrich younger people, enrichment of society may occur through creative or productive endeavors. Failure in this task results in self-indulgence and self-absorption.
8. Ego Integrity vs. Despair (50 and over)	As in the previous stages, the resolution of this stage is affected by the outcomes of the earlier crises. Here older people review and evaluate their lives. They come to terms with life, feeling that it has been lived the best it could have been and that it makes sense. The individual accepts responsibility for his or her life and has "adapted to its triumphs and disappointments" (Erikson, 1963, p. 268). Failing this ego integration, the person experiences regret and the feeling that life has been futile. Frequently there is the wish that it were possible to live life over again.

*Adapted from Erikson, 1963.

TABLE 4.2
Peck's Stages in Psychological Development in the Second Half of Life*

Stage	Description
Middle Age	
1. Valuing Wisdom vs. Valuing Physical Powers	There is a switch from an individual's primary self-definition based on strength, stamina, or attractiveness to a self-definition based on wisdom and experience (i.e., valuing "heads" over "hands").
2. Socializing vs. Sexualizing Human Relationships	Successful resolution on this issue means that, with diminished sex drive, older individuals are able to have a new depth of understanding in interpersonal relationships that was not possible when sex was a primary interaction.
3. Emotional Flexibility vs. Emotional Fixation	The capacity to shift emotional investments from one person to another person and one activity to another activity is crucial in the later years as parents die, then peers die, and children grow up and leave. Individuals who cannot resolve this dilemma have increasingly impoverished lives.
4. Mental Flexibility vs. Mental Rigidity	Mental flexibility is the capacity to keep an open mind and not get "stuck" in a fixed pattern of ideas or "rules." Closed minds emerge from lifetimes of experience, and although they have guided behavior in the past, they prohibit adaptive behavior in the later years.
Old Age	
5. Ego Differentiation vs. Work-Role Preoccupation	This represents an individual's successful switching from a primary identity linked to occupational or vocational roles, which are now no longer accurate, to involvement with one or more alternatives.
6. Body Transcendence vs. Body Preoccupation	The dilemma here is to go beyond preoccupation with age-related aches, pains, and disease processes. Success would involve transcending a focus on physical comfort and adopting a value system based on mental sources of pleasure.
7. Ego Transcendence vs. Ego Preoccupation	Failure at this level consists of a preoccupation with and dread of death, which would inhibit the last task of life—that is, to "make life more secure, more meaningful or happier for those that go on after one dies . . . Such a person would be experiencing a vital gratifying absorption in the future" (Peck, 1968, p. 91).

*Adapted from Peck, 1968.

TABLE 4.3
Loevinger's Stages of Ego Development*

Stage	Description
1. Presocial Stage 2. Symbiotic Stage	Babies must learn that they are separate from the environment (i.e., the self is distinguished from the nonself).
3. Impulsive Stage	Individuals are largely dependent upon and under the influence of their impulses. The child asserts his or her separate identity.
4. Self-protective Stage	The individual learns self-control, motivated by short-term self-gain and self-advantage.
5. Conformist Stage	The individual (usually in early adulthood) is characterized by the desire to live up to external definitions of good and bad and the expectations of his or her social group.
6. Self-aware Stage 7. Conscientious Stage 8. Individualistic Stage	During these 3 stages, the individual gradually becomes more introspective, acquires an internalized morality, feels guilty at transgressions, is aware of inner conflicts, and begins to have a greater tolerance for others.
9. Autonomous Stage 10. Integrated Stage	These last two stages are rarely attained. When they are attained, it is usually by adults in the later years. Individuals become increasingly more aware of their own dynamics, are self-accepting and are more able to deal with and resolve their own inner conflicts. They are occupied with self-fulfillment in a positive sense. In the 10th stage, they relinquish the unattainable and go beyond merely tolerating differences in others—to actually cherishing those differences. No longer seeking external definitions of who they are or who they should be, they explore their own individuality. Finally reaching a degree of comfort and security with the "self," the adult can turn outward, helping others in a humanitarian way.

*Adapted from Loevinger, 1976.

that each disappointment and sadness in life has something to teach.

Simon is another example of such potential for personal growth in old age. He too is beset, at age 97, by age-related physical problems. He is quite aware of his frailness, including periods of confusion, and yet it does not preoccupy him. Instead, he reads and studies, following his curious mind.

Months after I left Franklin Village, I returned to find Simon recuperating from a broken hip. He had very much enjoyed a psychotic reaction that was a side effect of pain medication for his hip. "In fact," he said, "I was sorry when the hallucinations left; they were most interesting!"

Annabelle seems to have entered the final, rarely achieved, stages in Loevinger's model. Although she feels that she has achieved enlightenment through a mystical experience, she appreciates that others have not. She respects that difference, perhaps even cherishes it, and keeps her revelations to herself so that others may "find enlightenment at their own pace."

Annabelle no longer evaluates, judges, and analyzes herself and others. She lives life effortlessly and seeks to help others with her unconditional comfort and support.

Not everyone is so evolved. Suzanne, our beloved "character," still struggles with Loevinger's hierarchical tasks. She has not relinquished the unattainable—that is, becoming a "lovely lady." Although she seems to do as she pleases, she feels guilty, still conflicted by external definitions of what she *should* be. Beth is also conflicted. She wrestles with acceptance. She grows impatient with other residents and with herself.

No doubt, living in Franklin Village facilitates personal growth for many residents. Old age and living in such a community frees residents from the consuming tasks that come with child-rearing and spousal caretaking. For example, the death of one woman's paralyzed husband ended her preoccupation with his care and ushered in the beginning of a new period of self-discovery.

At Franklin Village, there are none of the career pressures

associated with an achievement-oriented society. Although they may previously have been challenged, stimulated, or intrigued by such pressures, residents now report *relief* at being out of the "rat race." Their former passion for achievement is also diminished. For instance, one woman, who had written dozens of books, described her joy at "letting others do it now."

Residents have all of their basic needs satisfied within the community, which means that they have more opportunity and energy for personal growth and for helping others, a topic that we take up in the next chapter.

CHAPTER 5

HELPING

"Making a different ocean with just a little drop of water"

ALTRUISM

At 9 a.m. Beth and her friend Cynthia, a 78-year-old former secretary, looked like "everybody's grandma." At 9:05, a transformation began. They meticulously pinned back each strand of hair. Then they slathered gobs of white goo on their faces. "Cold cream," they said, "to protect the skin and make the cleanup easier." Next, Beth and Cynthia emptied their bags, spilling mirrors, tubes, and jars of greasepaint in red, blue, green, orange, and black and an assortment of rubber noses onto the table. There were oversized sunglasses and whistles and, of course, the wigs—a curly one that looked as if it had been an orange French poodle in a former life, one with bright red tufts sticking out every which way, and best of all, a rainbow wig with stripes of pink, yellow, green, and purple.

From that point on, Beth and Cynthia ceased to work in unison. Beth painted her eyebrows with peaks that gave her an expression of constant surprise, while Cynthia's downcast eyebrows made her appear timid and vulnerable. Beth painted red hearts on her chin and cheeks, while Cynthia favored a generous sprinkling of freckles.

At 10 a.m., they no longer were old ladies. Instead, they were clowns walking down the corridor of the Center, on their way to do what clowns do best—make people laugh, smile, and feel good. It was Friday, clowning day for Beth and Cynthia. They entered 20 nursing-care rooms. In each was an old person recuperating from an illness or incapacitated by poor mental or physical health. Some were dying and unable to speak. Nevertheless, every patient responded to the clowns—verbally, with gestures, or with a brightening of the eyes.

Once in the room, Beth and Cynthia made funny faces, joked, and performed tricks. If it felt "right," Beth placed a gold star on the back of a patient's hand and a kiss on the patient's cheek. Doctors and nurses paused at their work, if only for a minute, to laugh at their antics and smile approval.

At 12 noon they were, once again, two old ladies, wiping off greasepaint, the remnants of a tiring but invigorating morning. As they cleaned up, they discussed the new makeup and props they would buy and the new techniques and tricks they would learn.

"Why do you clown? It seems physically and emotionally draining," I asked. Beth (still the clown) answered, "I've been a fool all my life. Now I just put on whiteface." Then, in a more serious mood, she explained, "What else can I give them [the residents in nursing-care]? These are people who are dying. And besides, I get those 'magic moments' in return." Magic moments, Beth told me later, are experiences of "connection," a period of intimacy shared with another resident that makes it all worthwhile.

Although Beth and her friend are the only clowns, they are not the only people at Franklin Village who are kind and helpful to others. Hubert, for instance, helps a different group. He chooses to help the dull and lonely. Hubert's own popularity does not prevent him from noticing that there are residents who are not as lucky as he is. Periodically he feels guilty because he is not being as helpful to others as he thinks he should be.

There are three widowed men who seem especially lonely. They had led very "average" lives and are not particularly loquacious or entertaining. Therefore, they are not sought out as dinner partners. Every now and then, Hubert feels drawn to dine with them. He leads the conversation, is entertaining, and inquires about their activities. At the end of these meals, the men thank him for sitting with them and ask if he will do it again. The men relish his attention, which in turn makes Hubert feel good.

Although some residents are able to give money to charity organizations or social activist groups, most help in a way that is consistent with their talents, traits, or personalities. Beth, always the "fool," turns to clowning; Hubert, the socially gifted, uses his skill to warm the lonely and least popular. Andrew, an 83-year-old retired ophthalmologist, is another resident inclined to help. He has found a way to use his medical training that keeps him involved, in a limited but sufficient way, in the profession he loves. Andrew leads a Low Vision Group. Once a week, residents with impaired vision meet to hear him discuss various eye problems, treatments, current research, and practical hints about how to function with a visual impairment. He helps residents "translate" what their doctors say about medication and what surgery entails. "I try," he says, "to make the complex, simple, and the frightening seem routine." When residents must have medical or surgical treatment outside Franklin Village, Andrew drives them. When the time comes when he cannot drive, he will "go along for company" and to help where he can.

With helpful acts, the residents of Franklin Village demonstrate how much they value being useful. They say that helping others gives a sense of purpose or meaning to their lives. Yalom (1980) writes that life without meaning can be so unbearable that people suffer sometimes to the point of suicide. I remember one 76-year-old who knocked on the door of his 92-year-old neighbor every morning to inquire, "Is there anything I can do for you today?" Others have more ambitious goals: They want to help—or change—society and thus help the world.

THE QUAKER INFLUENCE

The entire board of directors and one-third of the residents of the community are members of the Society of Friends. The Quaker philosophy that pervades the community may provide a particularly nurturing context for the development and maintenance of altruism as well as for the personal growth discussed in Chapter 4.

The hallmark of the Quaker faith is the belief in equality. Quakers believe in "that of God in everyone." One person is no more godly or saintly or more blessed than any other person. Because they extend the belief of godliness to everyone, Quakers are committed to the cause of Native Americans, African Americans, the mentally disabled, and any other homeless, downtrodden, underdog, or minority group.

One Quaker resident told me that as a child she was taught, "Our lives are not our own. They are given to us to serve others." Children are encouraged to evaluate themselves on how well they are living up to their ideals. Such reflections may become lifelong habits. Hubert is an example of this. Regularly, he would feel guilty if he did not perceive himself as being helpful to others. This would motivate him to have dinner with the group of men who seldom had anyone join their table.

The Quaker philosophy reaches into the administration of the community in several ways. For example, under no circumstances are physical restraints ever used on residents. Restraints are considered an affront to the dignity of the sick or confused. Furthermore, residents are never forced to relinquish their apartments because someone believes that they are incapable of independent living. Residents move into the nursing facility only when they determine that they are ready. Finally, no one ever has to leave the community because he or she has run out of money. There is a fund to provide for these residents.

Hubert invited me to the next Meeting for Worship. It was on Sunday morning in the library at the Center. Six rows of chairs were placed in a large circle. A large bouquet of flowers was in the center of the room. I sat between Hubert and Beth, watching residents file in: Lynnette, Lily, Annabelle, Jeanette, Malcolm, and Andrew among them. The meeting "took up" at precisely 10:30 a.m.

Quakers worship silently.* They take their seats quietly and reverently. Some close their eyes and bow their heads; most try to relax their bodies so that they can focus on their inner world and spiritual self. The worshipper may meditate on a prayer, reflect on an experience, or ask God's help in choosing the right course. Silence and meditation create an atmosphere in which the worshipper may communicate with God (Kenworthy, 1988). The silence is broken only when the spirit moves a worshipper to rise and speak to the group. The theme usually has something to do with a Quaker concern (e.g., faith, raising children, love, caring, or compassion). When a person is finished speaking, he or she will sit down. The silence is resumed until someone else rises to speak. Quakers are expected to meditate and pray during the week so that something will well up within them during the Sunday meeting. Worshippers come to meeting "open to what happens" or prepared to respond "as way opens" (a Quaker expression).

Hubert was the first to speak. He said, "Throughout this past week, I have been thinking about priorities." He went on to say that in old age, long-term goals are not appropriate, but that even a single day is a gift that is worthy of goals and aspirations. Hubert sat down and another man rose to say, "This day will not come again. It's important to both enjoy it and to use it well [i.e., responsibly]." It was disconcerting to realize that my presence in the community and the questions I had been asking had spilled into Sunday worship. *One should not underestimate the impact of the researcher on the research.* In the same way, one should not

---

*In the eastern part of the United States, meetings are silent ("silent Friends"). The Midwest is the center for "pastoral Friends," whose services are more conventional, with a leader, singing, and formal prayer. There are only 200,000 Quakers in the world, 125,000 in the U.S. The religion was founded in England in 1652.

underestimate the impact of the Quaker philosophy on the helping behaviors of the Quaker and non-Quaker residents alike.

THE RECIPROCAL OBLIGATION

It would have been easy to spot Sylvia (an 81-year-old retired
hairdresser and owner of a chain of beauty shops) among the sea
of silver heads at Franklin Village. Sylvia is a "strawberry
blonde." However, I did not have to look for her. Sylvia found me
in the ladies' room at the Center. An assertive but friendly voice
from one sink over said, "You are the one studying aspirations,
aren't you? I'm interested in telling you about mine."

To say that Sylvia is unique doesn't tell enough. She stands out
among the reserved and genteel residents. For example, the
majority of residents wear glasses, but Sylvia's are *designer* frames
and her lenses are tinted pink. She wears bright red or green
blouses, while other women are more apt to wear soft pastels.
Her language is peppered with lively, colorful expressions that
have a Yiddish flavor. Sylvia said, "When I decided to go into a
retirement community, I made up my mind quickly. I don't futz
around."

Other apartments are decorated with old furniture. Antiques
are plentiful. Oriental rugs are common. Collections of artifacts
gathered from world travels are displayed on knickknack shelves
and tabletops. Colors tend towards the conservative. Sylvia's
apartment, on the other hand, is ablaze with color. Abstract art
hangs on her walls, and purple cushions adorn her sofa. Surfaces
are mostly Formica and objects are mainly Plexiglas or other
kinds of colorful plastics and ceramics. She has a minimum of
covering on the windows so that the sun streams in generously
to nourish green plants that sit in orange pots of different sizes
that are placed throughout the apartment.

At age 80, after 10 years of part-time classes, Sylvia graduated
cum laude from college with a degree in social work. At grad-
uation, she received a humanitarian award for her work with

poor African Americans and Hispanics. When asked about her award and the work she still does, she says, "I found out that I can do something about human suffering."

Sylvia knows about suffering personally. "I lost my mother at a young age, and when my father remarried, his new wife put my 14-year-old sister and me out on the street," she explains. "I was only 15 when my stepmother said there was no place for us in our father's house and our father said nothing. I know what it is to be penniless and have no one to turn to." Sylvia got a job as a "shampoo girl" in a beauty shop. Eventually she learned to be a hairdresser, bought her own shop, and then bought a whole chain of beauty shops. "But," she says, "I never forgot the help I received along the way. I knew that someday I would pay it back. I just didn't know when or how."

When Sylvia was 70, her closest friend, also 70, collapsed from a serious illness. The friend never regained her former vitality. She remained ill, constantly complaining and preoccupied with her body and its failings. Sylvia watched her old friend deteriorate. She was determined that this should not happen to her. Always an aficionado of self-help books, she sought out a professional counselor to ask, "How do I avoid what happened to my friend? How can I grow old in the best way?" He answered with five words: "You should go to school."

At first, Sylvia thought, "I can't go to college. I am too dumb." But her patrons and employees encouraged her to "give it a shot." Later they helped her edit her papers and study for exams. "I have never forgotten their help," she says.

College provided her with the training and the opportunities to "pay back" society for the help that she received over her life. She taught reading to inner-city youngsters whose parents were on probation and counseled socially isolated elderly people during her social work internship. Now, she teaches English to migrant farmworkers. In her spare time, she mends used clothing for distribution to third-world countries.

Sylvia, once a street-smart New York kid without education or the protection of parents, can vividly recall the feelings associated with being different, impoverished, and without hope. "When I first came to Franklin Village, all those old feelings returned. I don't have the same cultured background of most of the residents. I look different. I talk differently. I *am* different. It was hard for me to fit into this society, just like it is hard for poor kids or migrant farmers, who neither read nor speak English, to fit into society. For a time, I wasn't sure that I would make it here. But I used those feelings to figure out why I felt that way, and I overcame it. The miracle of life is that you *can* get over things. Nothing remains the same."

Robert, a 92-year-old retired accountant, helps his neighbors whenever he has the opportunity. For several hours each morning, he telephones residents who have health problems to make sure that they are okay and to find out if there is any task or errand that he can do for them.

Robert is not "paying back" for past kindnesses. Instead he is insuring the future. He believes that if he ever needs help, people will reciprocate his former acts of kindness. In the meantime, Robert enjoys life at Franklin Village. He is the oldest and best lawn-bowler on campus. He especially enjoys recalling his "youth" when he was "full of beans." That was when he was 70.

Sometimes, residents help others because it is part of their customary repertoire of behaviors, but it also has the secondary benefit—frequently recognized—of providing emotional reward to the giver. The Quaker environment and philosophy of the community encourages such behaviors. One woman told me that "service" had never been a part of her life. She said, "I don't want you to think that I was indifferent to the suffering of others, but helping just never entered my mind. Once I moved to this community, that changed, and I experienced a growing desire to help my neighbors."

Dowd (1980) writes that *social interaction*, in general, and social interaction among the aged, in particular, is basically an exchange process he calls *social exchange theory*. He writes that people help because they believe that the help they give is proportional to the help they receive or expect to receive. That expectation ensures that helping relationships will flourish. In a group of cleverly designed *field experiments*, Kahana and Midlarsky (1983) investigated helping behavior by subjects of different ages. They defined two types of help: (1) "sharing of the wealth," which is a *donation behavior* (the individual helps with money, time, or effort on behalf of another); and (2) "sharing of the pain," which is also called *rescue behavior* (here the cost is in discomfort or potential danger to the one who is doing the helping).

In the first experiment, malls and parks that were known to be frequented by a cross-section of individuals of diverse ages were selected as sites. Passers-by were given an opportunity to donate to a fund for children with birth defects. The plea was made compelling by displaying pictures of sad and crying children and their parents and by having a solicitor who appeared to be pregnant. People placed their donations in a canister that allowed for an undetected tabulation of the amount.

The results indicated that the frequency of giving increased with age through early adulthood. There was a plateau in mid-life, followed by another linear trend upward that was maintained through the retirement years. However, the *amounts* donated showed a different pattern. There was a linear trend throughout the life span until the age of 65, at which time there was a significant decline in the amount donated. In other words, more elderly people gave, but they gave less than the young. Because of the possibility that the differences were a reflection of variations in finances across the life span, another experiment was conducted.

The purpose of the second field experiment was to determine whether the elderly gave less because of their financial situations or whether they gave less because of an increasing disinclination to donate. This time, donation involved time and effort rather than money. A two-lever device replaced the canister. Subjects were told that if they wished to help the children, they should pull the lever marked "for the children" and a record would be made of the number of pulls. They were also told that local merchants had agreed to donate five cents to the fund for each pull of the lever marked "for the children."

Results of the second experiment indicated that the number of people at various ages who "donated" was similar to the first study. However, elderly people pulled the donation lever more frequently than younger people, and they pulled the unmarked lever less often than the younger subjects. Therefore, when the financial cost of donating was *controlled* (i.e., was consistent for all the subjects), elderly people gave more often and gave the highest donations.

The second series of experiments examined rescue-related behaviors. The first experiment explored the rates of voluntary enrollment for courses on first aid and cardiopulmonary resuscitation (CPR). When all were assured of adequate transportation to the classes, elderly people were significantly more likely to sign up for and attend classes than their younger counterparts.

More experiments were then conducted to measure *actual* rescue behavior. Again, subjects were of diverse ages. A situation was set up in which a person (age 30) required immediate medical help. Subjects (ages 18 to 85) who completed the first-aid course were compared with those who participated only in a neutral activity regarding responding to an emergency.

The results indicated that younger people generally are more likely to attempt to help. Nevertheless, among the older people, those who took the course were more likely to help than those who had not taken the course. It is noteworthy that when the degree of competence or effectiveness of the help was measured, trained older people were more likely to be *effective* helpers than untrained elderly and both trained and untrained younger people. The results of these experiments were interpreted as providing ample support for the *hypothesis* that older people are highly motivated to help and that the helping role may be highly "salient" or valued among the aged.

This seems to show that social exchange theory is only one aspect of helping in the later years. Kahana and Midlarsky (1983) write:

Providing assistance to others for altruistic reasons allows the older person to create his or her own intrinsic reward system without being dependent on reciprocity from others. Acts of altruistic help may thus serve to enhance self-esteem of the aged, and provide them with a sense of usefulness and meaning. (p. 359)

Such acts of elderly selflessness were understood by the philosopher Cicero as part of a circular reciprocity. He wrote about elderly peasant farmers who experienced great joy when they planted trees whose fruit they would never taste. In their own youth, they had benefited from fruit trees that they had not planted, and now—in their joyous act of fruit-tree planting—they were aware of participating in the eternal rhythms of the universe.

Older people are motivated to help and to give. They find both rewarding. The problem, however, is that they may not always have the *resources* (training, finances, or ability) to help. Monetary donations are an acceptable avenue, but not all elderly have discretionary funds.

Training for the elderly is an intriguing idea, but what kind of training, and for whom? This is an especially difficult question because even when older people already possess specific skills and knowledge, those resources are often perceived as less valuable because of the holder's age. The value of those skills is no longer self-evident; the skills must be demonstrated (Dowd, 1980). In an age-segregated community like Franklin Village, helpers do not have to "prove themselves." Help is given and received effortlessly. However, one cannot ignore the fact that a common religious background (which promotes service) is a motivating force for altruism among many residents and that all the friendly helping encourages more of the same.

Opportunity to show what they know or what they can do is rarely given to older people. Hubert is a perfect example. He has given "hundreds of speeches" but "no one calls anymore." He offers his talent to elementary school principals and "the lack of response hurts." Valentine (1992) suggests that one of the "higher purposes" in late life is an "inaugurative function" by which an older person wisely points the way for the less experienced. The relationship between Moses and Aaron illustrates this function. In the Old Testament, Moses brings his people through the Sinai, but—because of his various transgressions and because he has fulfilled his life purpose—he is forbidden to enter Canaan. So Moses goes to the edge of the desert and points Aaron (his "understudy") in the right direction.

Another more contemporary example of the inaugurative function can be seen in the "king-pin" of a successful family business, who gracefully repositions himself in the company to allow the young sons, daughters, nieces, and nephews to exercise their creativity and assume responsibility under the tutelage (not dictatorship) of the older self-made man or woman. The elder becomes a guide, advisor, and coach to the young, and thereby makes an even larger contribution than he or she has made before.

SOCIAL CHANGE

When Andrew is not busy with his many activities, he promotes recycling—encouraging others to protect the environment. He can be seen emptying the recycling bins that collect newspapers, aluminum cans, and glass bottles, or putting up posters urging residents to conserve energy and recycle.

One day I asked if he got frustrated with the limitations that his age had placed on him. He responded, "I realize that I can't do what I did before. Sometimes I wonder how I ever did it, but it doesn't matter. You want to know about aspiration? My aspiration is to make the world a better place. I can do that by being kind to neighbors or writing letters to politicians. It doesn't take much. It's as easy as making a different ocean with just a little drop of water."

Why do many older people aspire to make the world a better

place? Adler (1956) wrote that social interest indicates mental health and that the driving force behind it is the need to feel valuable. He wrote that one cannot exaggerate the impact that social interest can have on an individual's sense of well-being. The self-worth that develops from helping others fosters courage, an optimistic attitude, and greater acceptance of the human condition (e.g., the challenge of aging). In older people, social interest and social action help to shift their focus from their private pain and sense of personal injustice to a more satisfying position in which they are a useful part of the larger fellowship of humankind.

Although they have relatively little time left, residents seem to have an inordinate amount of patience. The ones who speak of social change feel empowered to change what grieves them and—unlike many younger people—they feel that no effort is too small or without meaning.

In the next chapter, the residents share their need and desire for intimate human contact or—social ties.

CHAPTER 6

SOCIAL TIES

"If you want a social life, don't just be interesting—be interested."

FAMILY

For decades, Marianne was the grande dame of the summer house at the New Jersey seaside. From Memorial Day to Labor Day, she welcomed weary relatives from the sweltering city. That family tradition nearly ended when Marianne's spinal cancer was diagnosed. With deep sadness, she announced that she was too ill to spend another summer at the shore.

The children would not hear of it. They insisted that Marianne spend her summer in the same way she had for 84 years. They packed up her wheelchair and all of her medications and carted Grandma off to the beach house. An elaborate schedule was worked out so that she would never be left alone. Younger relatives (including great-grandchildren) appeared regularly to spend their (perhaps last) summer holiday with Grandma.

"One by one, they came to take care of me," Marianne recalls. "When Jody came—she's a photography student—I dragged all the old tintypes from the attic. When I knew my oldest boy Bob was coming, I made sure I kept up with the newspapers that week. He loves to talk politics. I made their 'shifts' fun. One has to do interesting things with young people."

Marianne's aspiration is to remain *involved* in the lives of others. She says, "When I think about all that is happening in my family and in the world, it makes me want to stay around to see how everything turns out."*

The desire to have *intimate human contact* with others, especially family members, was voiced by men and women alike. Most residents exerted considerable energy to maintaining satisfactory relationships. They felt responsible for the strength of their family ties.

Ida, an 85-year-old homemaker, is an example of a resident who works at enhancing family relationships. The value of family was so important to her that she wanted to be certain it would be included in my study. Ida stopped me as I wandered through the Center, peering into activity rooms. "Are you the one," she asked, "who is studying aspirations?" As soon as I acknowledged that I was, Ida invited me into the quilting room. Ida said, "I want to tell you about family and how it is for old people with spouses and children."

We sat with other ladies around a large wooden frame. Stretched on the frame were two layers of cloth with batting stretched in between them. This was to be Ida's quilt. The top piece was made of 16 separate blocks that had been sewn together. Each one of the blocks had a different design constructed of brightly colored pieces of cloth. Ida threaded a long needle and began to outline the design with tiny stitches.

"Families must be together even when they are apart," she said. "Two of my granddaughters are traveling abroad. At this very moment, Mary is in Spain and Ellen is in Israel. I have the girls' itineraries—all the hotel names and addresses. Whenever they arrive in a new city, there is a letter from Grandma waiting for them at the hotel. No matter how far they travel, my letters

---

*The physical therapist at Franklin Village is convinced (although she can't prove it) that this attitude extends life. She has often witnessed what she calls the "just one more time" phenomenon. The very old or very ill will express the aspiration to "hang on" long enough to have a family-oriented experience "just one more time" (e.g., seeing a new grandchild, attending a wedding, or spending a holiday with a favorite child). The physical therapist is delighted when her patients do a "just one more time" six, seven, or even eight times.

keep them in touch with family news. They know about the good news and the problems. The letters keep thoughts of family in their minds."

"But husband keeping," said Ida, "is really my primary aspiration. My job is to keep my spouse alive and happy. Little has changed over the years. I am still responsible for the apartment and for the two meals a day that we have at home."

Bernadette (an 80-year-old former medical social worker) expressed a similar position just a few days later in the coffee shop. "I am the tail of the comet," she said. "I only wish to follow and support my husband."

Their words pushed my feminist buttons, so on both occasions I probed further. Ida and Bernadette are aware that their aspirations are unpopular with feminists. Bernadette put it succinctly: "I understand the views of young women, but I am comfortable with my life. It is consistent with the values of my upbringing. I don't feel oppressed, I feel lucky!" A male resident, Grover, had expressed the same attitude. "Labeling trees with their Latin names is just something I do to stay active. My wife," he said, "is my hobby."

Every aspiration to "keep up" with family and friends seemed to be accompanied by activity. For example, although normal physiological changes and age-related diseases can compromise the ability to drive safely, several residents aspired to drive (as long as possible) so that they could go visiting.* Even Jeanette, the 103-year-old blind woman, takes an active stance. She does not assume that relatives will visit her. She says, "People have to *want* to be with you. It's the same for any age. I care about the hobbies, the work, and the dreams of the young people on the staff at Franklin Village and in my family. If you want a social life, don't just be interesting—be interested."

Valuing family goes beyond nurturing the bonds between

---

*At present, most states do not provide a unified approach to assessing the skills of the older driver (Reuben, Silliman, & Traines, 1988). Driving helps one retain social ties. It also proves that one is a competent and functional adult (Eisenhandler, 1990). Thus, an older person might continue to drive despite the increased potential for serious injury or fatality to himself or herself and others.

relatives. Residents aspire to preserve and to improve the family's status, health, and wealth. Everyone has heard about people (old and young) who are compelled to clear the family name (when a family member has been unjustly accused of a crime). The tenaciousness with which they pursue exoneration (often for decades) attests to the strength of this kind of aspiration. Apparently, it is not always sufficient to bequeath money and heirlooms. Many residents spoke of the desire to enhance the family's well-being and ensure the continuity of the family unit.

In certain cultures, family well-being is even more valued than individual well-being. One of my students, a Chinese woman, had difficulty understanding Erikson's (1963) concept of the *identity crisis*. After hours of discussion, we realized that the problem was that in her culture, one has only *family* goals, not personal goals. For example, her study in America had nothing to do with her own wishes. She struggled with a foreign language and culture and with the academic demands of graduate school in order to bring honor to her family and to *improve* the family with her accomplishments.

Residents, at least in this stage of their lives, want to do the same. They work on projects that they believe will help younger members and draw the family closer. I suspect that many of the projects also give the older person a sense of immortality—that is, that the fruits of their labor will extend beyond their own lives.

Hubert, for instance, is one of the residents at Franklin Village who has such a project—a genealogy. He contacted the offspring of distant cousins for missing information, requested copies of birth and death certificates from towns he has never heard of, and poked around in relatives' attics looking for old Bibles (sometimes used to record the life events of their owners).

The genealogies constructed by residents range from simple family trees (listing several generations of relatives and their relationships) to Hubert's complex one that includes relocations, schooling, achievements, occupations, and hobbies. Among the items Hubert has collected are faded photographs, yellowed newspaper clippings of the famous and infamous, and copies of deeds for houses and businesses that are no longer standing.

Since retirement, Hubert has been thwarted in his efforts to contribute to society (e.g., his offer to give a talk to schoolchildren was ignored). He has no children or grandchildren; thus, he has little opportunity to enhance and nurture younger generations, a task Erikson (1963) saw as vital to healthy aging. His genealogy provides a vehicle to achieve that task. Everyone on his family tree will receive a copy to share and pass down long after Hubert is gone.

Ida's quilt is more than a pretty coverlet. It, too, is a history of a family. Each block represents significant events in the life of Ida's family (births, marriages, hardships, and joys). Each little piece of cloth has its own history. "That piece was from Great Grandma's wedding dress; this calico is from Mary's best Sunday dress; that's from Thomas's first pair of long pants; this is from the silk that Papa bought at the state fair. The memories are to be recounted to each generation of little ones before they go to sleep."

Malcolm, the retired social worker who was influenced by his grandfather's warning to "never let yourself go," collects inspirational readings that give him a spiritual lift. When his anthology is complete, he will pass it on to his children, providing them with a spiritual resource to use (once again) long after he is gone.

While Malcolm compiles spiritual readings and ponders man's relationship to God, his wife, Sonja (a 78-year-old former social worker), thinks about how a young wife might cope with an intrusive mother-in-law or how a shy child may be helped to feel more comfortable. She collects articles about the trials of family life and writes brief essays on family problems and solutions. Sonja intends to hand down her collection as well, hoping that it will provide guidance and support after she is gone. "My aspirations are oriented toward family," she said. "I feel responsible for providing some guidance, especially for keeping my dead sister's daughters 'on track.' I use every social-work skill I can muster to help them with their marriages and their child-rearing."

Sonja and others continue to accept the parental role, offering direction and instruction to the younger generation, despite the fact that their "children" are middle-aged or approaching old age. Some residents think that having children who are grand-parents themselves requires a major shift in family roles. They say that their children should now be equals—friends. Someday those same children might have to reverse roles and become parents to their parents. This was expressed as an aspiration—that is, adjusting to and helping family members adjust to relation-ship changes that must come about with the passage of time.

FRIENDS

A month before I moved to Franklin Village, I read an autobiographical account of a woman's experience of growing old. Near the end of the book, she wrote about preparing to enter a retirement community. I read with great interest because in just a few weeks I too would be moving to a retirement community to begin my study. You can imagine my surprise when she gave the name of the community—Franklin Village.

Shortly after I arrived in the community, I discovered that the writer, Marjorie (an 85-year-old retired teacher and author), was alive and well and still living at Franklin Village. I called her to arrange an interview. Marjorie turned out to be a real-life "Anna" from *Anna and the King of Siam*. I listened to her life story and tried to envision what she looked like at 40, when she was tutor to the prince of an exotic kingdom. I could almost hear refrains from "Getting to Know You" playing in the background.

"When I arrived at the palace for the first time," she said, "the chamberlains told me that the crown prince had been instructed to say: 'It is very good of you to come so far to teach me.' I was told to respond: 'It is very good of you to welcome me so kindly.'"

However, Marjorie had sent the prince a box of candy from

America—something that was scarce in his country, even for a prince. When the 12-year-old prince entered the room, he did not utter the prepared statement. Instead, he said, "Thank you for the candy." "I knew right then that we would get along quite well," she said.

After her four-year stint as English teacher to the prince, Marjorie resumed her work in America and her travels around the world. She wrote 29 books, 15 of them for children. She enjoyed an exciting career but is pleased to "let others do the writing and teaching now." She no longer publishes, but continues to keep her personal journal. She no longer travels, but is content to read about the travels of others. She continues to correspond with her "little prince," who is a grown man with his own family. Her biggest pleasure—one she aspires to continue—is enjoying the company of beloved *friends*. Aspirations to stay active or experience pleasure become easier to accomplish when one has a friend with whom to do things.

Stella, Marjorie's dearest friend, lives a mile and a half from Franklin Village. They talk frequently on the telephone, especially during the cold winters when Marjorie limits her outings to daily treks to the Center dining room. When spring arrives, the women pack sandwiches, little cakes or fruit, and containers of hot tea. If they start out at the same time and do not stop to chat with anyone along the way, they end up meeting exactly halfway between their two homes. They unfold a blanket and spread out their picnic lunch.

The relationship between Stella and Marjorie spans 50 years and is typical of long-standing friendships between older people. When they are together, the passage of time is irrelevant. When they look at each other, they do not see the faces of old women. They are as they always were—two teachers discussing former students and shared experiences. In this way, friends (in old age) maintain a sense of continuity, preserve one another's self-image, and confirm each other's sense of worth (Jerome, 1981).

Friendship provides an arena in which to "play out" many of the aspirations expressed by the elderly residents of Franklin Village. Residents who value helping assist friends who become ill or disabled. They provide comfort for the grieving, empathy for the distressed, and opportunities for the exchange of confidences.

Jerome (1981) points out that *new* friends are especially important for elderly who are interested in personal growth. With new friends, one can try out "a new way of being" without the feelings of resistance that may characterize long-standing friends (who are more comfortable with the "old" self).

Friends may be empathic listeners to a life review. It is easier to share a life review with friends than with family members who might have a vested interest in denying, repressing, or avoiding sensitive issues (Lewittes, 1988).

Many males in this cohort are at greater risk of becoming friendless simply because they have come out of childhood with fewer relationship skills. When a man's wife was his only intimate friend, her loss may place him at greater risk for becoming socially isolated because of a limited pool of friends. However, his chances of finding a new mate is greater than it is for widows. It is likely that male friendships will become more common in future generations as gender roles are loosened and male sensitivity becomes more valued.

What is unlikely to change is the tremendous sense of loss experienced when friends die. As a result, people often become wary about making new friends. Marjorie said, "It is hard to make new friends at Franklin Village when you know they might die too. Even when they don't die before you do, it is difficult to maintain relationships in the face of poor health, hearing and vision problems, and diminished mobility."

In the future, friendship is likely to become even more important to the well-being of the elderly than it is now. Longevity and smaller families translate into fewer children and grandchildren to provide care for the elderly. Older adults (especially the childless and those who survive their offspring and their spouses) will increasingly rely on each other for emotional and physical support.

SOCIAL TIES AND WELL-BEING

Adler (Ansbacher & Ansbacher, 1956) said that an individual who is well adjusted "feels at home in life" (p. 155). Gerontological researchers refer to this sense of well-being as *successful aging*, *high morale*, *psychological well-being*, or *life satisfaction*.

Although the professional literature on psychological well-being in the second half of life is extensive, there is little information about whether the indicators of well-being developed for research purposes fit the values and experiences of those to whom they are applied (Ryff, 1989). For example, most measures dwell on the past rather than the present, suggesting that the present state of being is determined by past experiences.

One study, however, was unique, in that the researchers directly asked 69 middle-aged (age 30 to 64) and 102 older (age 65 +) men and women to define positive psychological functioning in adulthood (Ryff, 1989).*

Among the questions Ryff asked was: "What is most important to you in your life at the present time?" The subjects answered most frequently in terms of family (e.g., spouses, children). Another question asked: "What does it mean to be well adjusted?" To this, the most frequently occurring answer was "other oriented" (emphasizing good relationships with others and caring about others). Ryff also asked: "How would you define the ideal person?" The most frequent answers were "kind, does things for others" and "relates well to people." The men and women in both groups (middle-aged and old) associated the interpersonal realm with positive functioning and well-being.

Marianne, Ida, Bernadette, and Grover would probably agree that having family and friends to do things with and to care

---

*Although the older community-dwelling subjects in the study were somewhat younger on average (73 years old) than residents at Franklin Village (81 years old), they were similar in other ways—that is, they were relatively healthy, economically comfortable, and well educated.

about is important and helps them to feel good. Ryff suggests that what people claim is important to them (i.e., their values) may be the standard by which they judge their own lives and thus may help researchers to understand the essential features of positive aging. If social ties are important to most older people, what might happen when older people are deprived of social relationships?

SOCIAL TIES AND HEALTH

In Chapter 3, Alton and Grover espoused the conventional wisdom that *staying busy keeps one healthy*. This belief motivates a great deal of the activity at Franklin Village. I never heard any residents say that *maintaining ties with family and friends keeps one healthy*, but clearly a great deal of energy is directed to this end.

There is an accumulating body of evidence showing that social relationships influence health. Individuals with poor or limited social relationships tend to be less healthy (psychologically and physically) and more likely to die. The lack of social relationships constitutes a health risk that is as great as smoking, obesity, or lack of exercise (House, Landis, & Umberson, 1988). Social relationships enhance immunity, increase the likelihood that individuals will adhere to health-related behaviors, and maximize adaptation and recovery from illness (Bloom, 1982; Cobb, 1976; Doehrman, 1977).

In the last 20 years, there has been a burgeoning of research about social networks and social supports (see Ell, 1984, for a review of the literature). A *social network* consists of all of an individual's social contacts. This includes family, friends, neighbors, coworkers, and formal helpers such as the retirement community staff or physicians. Network ties can be close-knit (intimate relationships) or loose-knit (casual acquaintances). Social networks may, over time, change in size, source of ties, member homogeneity, frequency of contacts, and opportunity for reciprocal exchange between members (Ell, 1984).

A social support system, on the other hand, is a subset of people within an individual's social network on whom that individual can rely for support (Thoits, 1982). The people who are in one's social support system supply emotional support, advice, guidance, feedback, material aid, and services (Ell, 1984). Social support is more difficult to measure than social networks because any measure of social support must first assess a need for support and then establish evidence that support was exchanged in response to that need (Lubben, 1988). Unfortunately, the professional literature has suffered from a lack of clarity between the two terms (Ell, 1984). In addition, quantity versus quality of relationships has emerged as an important, but not clarified, consideration.

To date, the link between social ties and health remains unclear. The most common explanation is that social ties provide a *buffering effect* from stress—that is, relationships moderate the potentially deleterious health effects of negative life events (Cassel, 1976; Cobb, 1976).

A second theory suggests that social support favorably and directly impacts health by *encouraging compliance with positive health behaviors and the cessation of negative practices* (Crawford, 1987). For example, family and friends frequently encourage loved ones to take better care of themselves. They might also urge and facilitate timely medical attention and provide health information.

Another theory states that in the presence of illness, social support (intimate, confiding relationships) enables one to cope more effectively, thereby *speeding adaptation and recovery* (Cohen & Syme, 1985).

The final theory is that the absence of social ties in a person's life may have a *direct physiological effect* on their health status (House, Landis, & Umberson, 1988). There are research findings that suggest that variations in exposure to social contacts produce physiological effects that could, if prolonged, cause serious illness and even death. For example, the presence of familiar people has been shown to reduce anxiety and physiological arousal in humans in potentially stressful laboratory situations (Back & Bogdonoff, 1967).*

Although social ties include both family and friends, recent studies suggest that each type of relationship may make a unique contribution to the well-being of older people (Larson, Mannell, & Zuzanek, 1986). For most noninstitutionalized elderly people, family members provide physical security and emotional support—that is, they carry out most caregiving tasks. Friends, on the other hand, tend to provide something that may be more valuable to a sense of well-being—fun. "The levity and spontaneity of friends create a context in which older adults more readily transcend the constraints of daily existence" (Larson, Mannell, & Zuzanek, 1986, p. 122).

In the next chapter, residents tell about other sources of fun—and the importance of pleasure in their daily lives.

---

*This effect might operate across species. Affectionate petting can reduce the cardiovascular sequelae of stressful situations among dogs, cats, horses, and rabbits (Lynch, 1979). Preliminary evidence also indicates the health benefits of pets for the isolated elderly (Goldmeier, 1986).

CHAPTER 7

PLEASURE

"We have all come here to die, but why not enjoy ourselves while we're waiting for that to happen?"

OLD AGE, PASSION, AND PLEASURE

The room was virtually humming with the bantering and philosophizing of 13 white-haired men and women. With so many residents gathered in one place and the conversation so animated, my fear of missing something important drove me to break my "no note-taking" rule. My pencil fairly raced across a yellow pad as I tried to capture every quotable remark and poignant anecdote.

The summer and the study were drawing to a close. I had organized this *focus group* so that I could include the thoughts of several more residents in the short time remaining. The members of the focus group were typical Franklin Village residents. They were:

Gregory, an 85-year-old retired financial administrator
Carol (Gregory's wife), a 77-year-old former museum curator
Dinah, an 82-year-old former teacher
Elaine, a 79-year-old retired social worker
Lester, a 77-year-old former research scientist
Nina (Lester's wife), an 81-year-old former teacher

Peter, an 81-year-old former research scientist
Verna (Peter's wife), a 78-year-old former translator
Fritz, a 77-year-old retired businessman
Jessica (Fritz's wife), a 78-year-old former teacher
Gladys, an 83-year-old former guidance counselor
Barton, an 83-year-old retired physician
Emily (Barton's wife), a 76-year-old former director of hospital
       volunteers

Emily was one of the first to speak. She said that although she still had aspirations, much of her youthful passion had disappeared. "When you are old," she said, "your energy is lower. You still *want* to do things, but you don't suffer as much if you can't do them." "Initially," she said, "old people fret about not being able to do the things that they used to do quite easily. Everyone goes through it. When people move into this community, their *thermostat* is usually high. Eventually the thermostat [the desire to do things] gets adjusted according to one's capacity, and the fretting subsides."

Everyone agreed that passion fades with age, but Barton disliked Emily's thermostat metaphor. "A thermostat," he said, "implies that we have some control when, in fact, we have no control over the amount of desire we maintain for our former activities and aspirations."

Gregory offered himself as an example of what it feels like to have a thermostat that refuses to adjust. "Going from *wanting* to do everything to being relieved not to *have to* do everything sounds good, but I for one am having trouble with it. Just talking about it makes my arthritis act up."

Carol chimed in, "Sometimes my pride hurts because I can't do what I used to do, but the rest of the time I am content not to have my former passions—and relieved not to feel guilty about that." Heads nodded knowingly.

"The answer might be to trade in old aspirations for new, 'lower type' aspirations," offered Jessica. "Maybe you cannot play a musical instrument as well as before, but you can always try a less demanding instrument or—if that's not possible—listen to other people's music. It may be less satisfying, but nevertheless gratifying."

I asked the group, "Should older people have aspirations?" Lester blurted out, "It is deadly if we don't! At this age it would be silly to have long-term aspirations, but we can plan a year or two ahead."

"How about a few weeks?" added Nina. "My only aspiration is to mend my broken leg and get out of this wheelchair."

"It is important to have aspirations and to work on them, but it is not necessary to achieve them," volunteered Elaine. "For example, I wanted to learn to weave. I tried, but I could not pick it up. However, I had pleasure trying."

Peter picked up on the reference to pleasure. "Ah, pleasure," he said. "Let's be brutally frank. We have all come here to *die*, but why not enjoy ourselves while we are waiting for that to happen?"

For a few moments, the room was still. Then Fritz got the conversation going again by sharing the pleasures of golf. Peter followed by telling how good it was to spend hours each day doing nothing but reading.

Although the pursuit of pleasure is part of the American way of life, it is not usually valued in American culture. Old people receive mixed messages from our society. They are told, for instance, to stop working and to *enjoy* their leisure time, but then they are made to feel that if they do that, they are unproductive and socially useless (Dytchwald & Flower, 1989).

Before telling me about pleasure aspirations, residents would often mention their achievements and altruistic deeds, as if to demonstrate that they had "earned" the right to enjoy themselves. This makes sense when we realize that the Protestant work ethic orientation is that leisure (and the pursuit of pleasure) is worthwhile only when it allows people to rest so that they can return to work. In contrast, ancient Greeks viewed leisure not as a necessary respite from work but as a desirable end in itself. In other words, work was the necessary evil to achieve leisure.

Pleasure was also mentioned by the residents I call "recreationalists," "relaxers," "artists," "aesthetes," "re-creators," and "maintainers."

Recreationalists and Relaxers

Robert, the resident who is confident that his friends will eventually reciprocate his acts of kindness, has a contagious smile, a bald head with a noticeable shine, and no shoulders. The first time I saw him, I wondered if shoulders, like arches, could fall, and if this was some age-related malady I had never heard of. Not having shoulders makes Robert's arms appear unnaturally long. Robert also leans to the left when he walks, his long arms swinging at his sides. His left arm is lower than his right.

Unlike most of the male residents, Robert seems to favor striped polo shirts (of the type worn by small boys) and short pants that show off a pair of spindly bowed legs. Robert is well known at Franklin Village—for his athletic prowess.

Robert's English bowling team practices three times a week and competes with other teams at Franklin Village once a week. During practice, the players tease one another about the quality of their "rolls." The game requires bending, stretching, and arm-swinging. Robert is both the oldest and the best player in the Franklin Village league. "I used to travel from 'here to there' with my wife when I was young. Now I just want to live another day. All I really want to do is relax and bowl," he says.

Warren, an 82-year-old retired real estate appraiser, and his wife Aileen, an 85-year-old former interior decorator and real estate broker, share Robert's desire to relax. They say that after 65, one should not aspire to anything. Although they still travel, play bridge, and work on committees, they look forward to the time when they "will do nothing." The only way they can explain their lack of desire to do more is "energy decline." Warren explains, "From the age of 80 to 85, you go down fast."

Albert, a 100-year-old former pharmacist, is another resident of some notoriety. Albert's 100th birthday celebration was so grand that it sent him to the hospital for two weeks to recuperate. "It was an aspiration that I achieved," he says. "My father lived to 95 and my mother to 85. If my father could live a long life, so could I. Someone once lived to 130. If they could do it, so can I. My new aspiration? A hundred and one, of course."

Most of Albert's notoriety comes from his attention to birthdays. Once a year, for the last 10 years, he has thrown a gigantic party for residents who have passed 90. Last year, there were 50 residents over 90 at Franklin Village. Thirty-nine came to the shindig.

As soon as Albert's doctor gives him permission, he will resume his formidable schedule—billiards (once a week), bowling (three times a week), and putting on the putting green and playing bridge (each four times a week).

We might call Robert and Albert *recreationalists*—retirement community members whose primary social role is that of participation in leisure-time activities (Osgood, 1983). They identify themselves as bowlers or golfers and take pride in their skills. The pleasure of the mastery and the respect they receive from other residents is highly valued.

The *relaxers*, on the other hand, enjoy the simple pleasures. Most of all, they read, if they like, and notice things they haven't had time to enjoy before.* Recreationalists and relaxers have mellowed. No longer do they have *superegos* that tie up a lot of energy censoring impulses to "go fishing" when there is work to be done. They use their energy to play or merely to relax.

Artists

Victoria is an 80-year-old former advertising writer. Except for the past three years (the time she has lived in Franklin Vil-

---

*The relaxers are not to be confused with what Osgood (1983) calls the retirees—that is, the people who, because of failing health, have "retired from life" (p. 37).

lage), she has been obsessed with a single unfulfilled aspiration—"to paint and nothing else."

Her aspiration developed when she was a junior in college. Unable to take the writing course she wanted, Victoria enrolled in an art history course despite the fact that she knew nothing about art. "The professor was so exciting and interesting," she says. "I developed an ambition to paint."

Victoria recounts a tumultuous and unhappy life. She had a father who abused her and an alcoholic husband who also abused her. She became successful on Madison Avenue but hated the work. As the breadwinner of the family, she never had time to paint or money to buy lessons and supplies. She always felt trapped by responsibilities, an abusive relationship, and a job she dreaded.

At Franklin Village, Victoria finally has the opportunity to paint, but conventional wisdom tells us that at age 80, she is not likely to produce many works nor anything of merit. (Of course, there are always exceptions to this, like Grandma Moses, who began painting at age 76.) After all, creativity is like skiing. Some believe that if you don't start young, you can't expect much. Since decline in creative powers begins around mid-life, most people would advise Victoria not to count on being a "serious" artist.

There does seem to be an age curve in the *number* of creative contributions made by creative people. Many artists start in their 20s, peak in their 30s and 40s, and then experience a gradual decline after 40. The placement of the peak varies according to the domain. Some fields—for example, lyric poetry—are characterized by early peaks and steep descents, whereas other fields of artistic endeavor, such as novel writing, have later ascents, late peaks, and minimal descents (Simonton, 1988).

Nevertheless, age curves don't describe the full picture. The creative drive may motivate the elderly person to continue despite adversity. For example, in their final years, Beethoven composed masterpieces while deaf, Renoir had to have his paintbrush tied to his hand because of disabling rheumatism, and

Matisse worked from his wheelchair with a crayon attached to a bamboo pole. As for quality, there is no indication that the elderly have a different quality ratio (number of poor works to number of fine works produced) than creative people of other ages (Simonton, 1990).

Victoria is what is known in creative circles as "a late bloomer." A creative career unfolds over time; in other words, if people start late, they peak late. Simonton (1990) more recently writes that "the age curve is really not an age curve at all, but rather a career curve" (p. 628). A late starter may maintain a higher output longer than an early starter. In addition, empirical research suggests that a second peak, a "swan song,"* frequently occurs in the final years (Simonton, 1989).

Brushes, paint, and canvases fill Victoria's rooms. Her apartment is more like a sparsely furnished studio than the living quarters of an old woman. She says, "The three years that I have lived in Franklin Village have been all joy and productivity. I have painted more canvases in the last three years than I have in the past 50. A gallery wants to put on a one-woman show. Imagine that!"

Aesthetes

Aesthetes are people who possess a special appreciation of what is beautiful and endeavor to carry ideas of beauty into everyday life (The Oxford English Dictionary, 1989). Dora, a 72-year-old former teacher, is an aesthete. "Franklin Village takes care of my body and my soul," she says. Alarmed by the situations of several friends who were "wiped out" by catastrophic illness in their final years, Dora feels safe from such destitution at Franklin Village.

Her soul is nourished, she says, by the natural beauty of the community and its proximity to a botanical garden. "The small

---

*According to folklore, a swan sings once in its life—as death approaches (Kastenbaum, 1991).

price of a pass to the gardens brings me countless hours of the pleasure of beauty," she says.

Other residents, like Grover, value the beauty of order—in their gardens, in their possessions, and in the pattern of their lives. Grover's aspirations were echoed throughout the study: "I would love to sort through and organize years and years' worth of photos and slides." Some residents had started this ordering; others look forward to "starting it soon," while still others admitted that they probably would never accomplish this goal.

Re-creators

Pleasure comes in many forms in the community. When certain residents recalled their childhoods, they also expressed a desire to re-create (as far as they were able) some of the experiences from their earlier life.

One morning at breakfast, Beth introduced me to Audrey, a 75-year-old retired scientist. As usual, I explained my presence in the community. Audrey responded, "My aspiration is to sleep." She explained that she had a problem with sleeping too much. A good part of her day was spent in bed. No one had been able to help her with this affliction.

Audrey and I continued to talk. Ever since she was a child, she had longed to become an architect. Her parents could not afford to send her to architecture school. Chemistry was cheaper, so Audrey became a chemist. She maintains the dream, despite her age. She knows, of course, that she will never become an architect, but she reads the professional journals anyway, draws blueprints, and fantasizes. Her eyes sparkled as we talked. Later, Beth said that she had never seen Audrey so open and verbal. It was rare to draw her out of her sleepiness.

Arthur, a 72-year-old retired Wall Street financial consultant, and his wife, Edith, a 67-year-old homemaker, re-create past experience, not only in fantasy, but in their everyday life. As children, Arthur and Edith grew vegetables that they took to market. They garden now, not because of need, but to recapture the feelings and thoughts they had as children, growing and selling their produce. Edith preserves jellies from the raspberries and cherries. She says, "It is a joyful re-creation of things past."

Others reflect on their youth but see instead partial learnings and unfinished tasks. They aspire to re-create these events so that they can finally enjoy completing what they did not complete earlier.

Matthew, the 74-year-old engineer, wants to "brush up" on his French. He studied French as a youngster, but regrettably devoted little time to it. He also wants to learn about nature. He says, "I never spent much time on it when I was a youth. Now I want to go back and learn the names of things."

Benjamin, a 76-year-old retired physician, wants to "go back" and study history and nature. Now that he is a grown man, these subjects hold a new interest for him, especially since, as he says, he doesn't have to be examined in them.

The original experience often happened 60 or 70 years earlier. Nevertheless, people's feelings of longing (e.g., wanting to be an architect), pride (e.g., growing vegetables and contributing income to the family), and regret (e.g., for unfinished tasks) were retained over time and continued to influence their thoughts, activities, and aspirations.

Maintainers

Some residents are interested only in maintaining the pleasure they derive from the present. They spend little time recalling the past or aspiring to the future. They are content with the status quo.

For example, Constance, a former secretary, is vehement. "I haven't developed a new interest since I moved to Franklin Village 15 years ago, and I do not want to start now." At 87, she desires only to continue to participate in the activities that always

gave her pleasure. Her walls in the nursing facility are covered
with awards of recognition for years of community service.

Fred, a 71-year-old retired chemical engineer, and his wife,
Pauline, a 70-year-old former museum guide, also focus on keeping things the same. They are unusual in that they claim that the
only thing that has changed for them in the seven years since
moving into the community is their address. They maintain
their friendships outside the community and insist on shopping
in the same stores.

Donald, a 72-year-old retired businessman and railroad buff,
wishes to continue with the hobby that has occupied most of his
time for the past two years. Donald and another resident started
The Franklin Village Railroad Club. Members build, expand,
and develop a most unusual model railroad, which is housed in
the lower level of the Center. The railroad is H.O. gauge (1 foot
to 87 feet in scale). Members may work on building track, sce-
nery, or individual railroad cars. Others are trained to operate
the railroad, which is run only once a month.

There are 77 "passive participants" in the club. Each one is
responsible for at least one railroad car. First, he or she has to
recall a memory associated with a train. Each car on the train
represents one of these memories. A personal characteristic or a
resident's name may be memorialized with a railroad car. For
example, one resident is named Phoebe. When she was a young
girl, she was teased about being "Phoebe Snow." She had no idea
what that meant until she got older and discovered that it was the
nickname of a passenger train that was painted snow-white to
demonstrate that the locomotive burned "clean" anthracite coal.
She now has a car on the model railroad called the Phoebe Snow,
an exact replica of one of the original cars.

One man remembered when, as a young boy, he had to
accompany four horses across several states in a boxcar. Now
there is a replica of that boxcar, with four tiny horses inside, on
the model railroad. Another resident remembered how as a child
he used to take frequent train rides. One day, he climbed atop
a car to get some fresh air. He got locked out of the car and had

to sit for three hours on top of the train. That train car is re-created, complete with a miniature boy sitting on top of it.

The Railroad Club keeps a scrapbook. Each memory is recounted in the book, along with a picture of the model train car that represents it.

Although these residents aspired to keep life the same, and some even claimed that it was the same as always, most were aware of the "constraints of age" and of subtle differences. Nevertheless, their perception was of the pleasurable continuity to their lives that they wished to maintain as long as possible.

Chinen (1991) writes that an ideal goal for the later years is the return of childlike wonder and delight with everyday life, when even small events elicit great pleasure. To illustrate, he recounts the writings of psychoanalyst Martin Grotjahn (1982):

> I don't work anymore. Peculiarly enough, I feel well about it. . . . I sit in the sun watching the leaves slowly sail across the waters of the swimming pool. I think, I dream, I draw, I sit—I feel free of worry—almost free of this world of reality. If anyone had told me that I would be quietly happy just sitting here, reading a little, writing a little, and enjoying life in a quiet and modest way, I, of course, would not have believed. That a walk across the street to the corner of the park satisfies me when I always thought that a four-hour walk was just not good enough: that surprises me. (p. 234)

SEXUAL PLEASURE IN LATE LIFE

Whenever I think about sexuality in late life, I am reminded of Suzanne's joke (page 70) in which a scientist asks an older man if he still has sex. The man gleefully acknowledges that he *is* sexually active—"once a year." The punch line eventually reveals that the man is happy, despite the infrequency, because "Tonight's the night!"

Suzanne's joke captures the essence of several ageist stereotypes and myths while, at the same time, it reveals a truth or two. The belief that people normally lose sexual interest or the capacity for sexual enjoyment with advanced age is a misconception that becomes a self-fulfilling prophecy for many elderly. The Duke Longitudinal Studies* indicate that sex continues to play an important role in the lives of men and women well into their 70s (Palmore, 1981). Many older adults report that sex is at least as satisfying as it was when they were younger, and, in some cases, it is more satisfying than it had been (Starr & Weiner, 1981).

Sexual interest, sexual enjoyment, and sexual functioning may fluctuate at *any* age for a plethora of complex physical and psychological reasons, including boredom, excessive eating or drinking, depression, and fear of failure. Many of the conditions described below, which are more common in the second half of life, are not exclusive to those years and do not automatically result in the end of sexual pleasure.

Changing physiology

Sexual organs may not work the same way they used to. Older men may voice concern because it takes longer to achieve erections than it used to, and the erections are not as firm as in younger days. There is also a reduction in the volume of seminal fluid, and a longer period must pass before an ejaculation is possible again. However, Butler, Lewis, and Sunderland (1991) wisely point out that while older men may take longer to obtain an erection and achieve ejaculation, they tend to have more control over the pressure to ejaculate and are thus able to make love longer before coming to orgasm (a quality often greatly appreciated by partners).

---

*The Duke Longitudinal Studies are two large-scale studies that focus on providing information that describes normal aging. The first study began in 1955 with 270 subjects (ages 60 to 94). The second study began in 1968 with 502 subjects (ages 46 to 70). Data collection on both studies was completed in 1976.

Older women commonly experience a thinning of the vaginal walls and consequent pain or bleeding during intercourse (a condition certain to diminish sexual activity). The vagina may also shrink in length and width; lubricating vaginal secretions may decrease. Although the use of long-term hormone-replacement therapy to alleviate these conditions is controversial, short-term courses of small doses of combinations of female hormones have helped many women.

Emotional distress

Bereavement, the loss of health or social roles, adjustment to retirement, or worries about children, finances, or health can interfere with sexual interest, desire, and functioning. People who are angry with their partners or who have difficulties accepting the physical changes that come with aging bodies may find their sexual desires waning, and they may choose to permanently relinquish that part of their lives. One of the major problems for older men, in particular, is fear of impotence, which occurs on occasion in most men's lives. Ironically, the anxiety generated by the experience may then contribute to a more permanent impotency.

Chronic illness

Chronic illness can directly and indirectly interfere with sexuality. Heart disease is an excellent example. Many older adults give up sex after a heart attack because they mistakenly believe that sexual activity at their age and with their medical history would be akin to bungee-jumping. In fact, most experts believe that if patients abstain for 8 to 14 weeks after a heart attack, and if they can walk briskly for three blocks without distress in the chest, palpitations, or shortness of breath, they are then well enough for sexual exertion (Butler & Lewis, 1988). Likewise, moderate hypertension need not restrict sexual activity, although severe hypertension may require some modifications. Diabetes can cause chronic impotence in men, although sexual interest and desire may continue. A stroke may seriously impair a person's ability to perform but does not necessarily damage sexual desire.

Medications

A number of drugs have the potential to interfere with sexual desire and performance (including drugs used to treat some of the disorders mentioned above). These include tranquilizers and antidepressants. Medications used to treat hypertension are especially suspect when sexual problems are reported. Alcohol may also interfere with sexual performance in both men and women. It is believed, for example, that 80% of male heavy drinkers have serious problems with impotence, sterility, or loss of sexual desire (Butler & Lewis, 1988).

A new penile erection treatment has helped many couples resume sex lives which were halted by the side effects of medication, chronic illness, or surgery. This exciting new technology (combined with psychological counseling) has also been successful in the treatment of penile erectile dysfunction that is rooted in emotional distress (Wagner & Kaplan, 1993; Eid & Pearce, 1993).

In Suzanne's joke, sexuality among the aged was a topic for research, suggesting that it is not well-understood and is worthy of attention. There is a great deal of confusion in this area. We tend to assume that old people are asexual, so when they display sexual interest, we react with shock and dismay. For example, a social worker told me about a situation in which she had twice hired aides to provide some light housekeeping and personal-care services for her client, "Mr. James," an elderly stroke patient. One after another, the young aides quit the job, complaining that Mr. James was "a dirty old man." Upon investigation, the social worker discovered that Mr. James (in his 70s and physically disabled) still had a robust interest in sex. The personal care (including bathing) had sexually aroused him. He then mistakenly interpreted his aides' warmth and friendliness as evidence of mutual interest and possible receptiveness to his sexual advances.

It is not uncommon in cases like this to assume than an older man (and a disabled one, at that) would not or should not be sexually aroused. Or, if arousal occurs, there is a tendency to attribute it to dementia. We would not make the same assumptions and judgments if a 28-year-old man was being bathed and cleaned by an attractive attendant. The remedy is simple: Sexuality needs to be discussed with the older client and included in the training of all professional and paraprofessional caregivers.

On the other hand, Western society glorifies sexual heroics. This makes old people think something is wrong with them if they don't have strong sexual desires, when, in fact, they may never have had hearty sexual appetites. After a long history of sexual or relationship problems, some people may simply be relieved that age offers a convenient "out."

Frequently, diminished sexual interest or sexual activity represents an individual's adjustment to a lack of opportunity. The elderly man in Suzanne's joke appears to have made a healthy adjustment in his sexual life. His infrequency might be an accommodation to low energy, a variety of health problems, or perhaps the unavailability of willing partners. Nevertheless, his enthusiasm and capacity for sexual pleasure remains high.

It is a myth that sexual intercourse is the only fulfilling or "real" sex. This is particularly relevant for the elderly, some of whom lose their partners to death or to dementia. Alzheimer's disease, for example, slowly causes deterioration in its victims to the extent that the sufferer is no longer "the same person." Instead of an adult-to-adult relationship (which includes sexuality), the relationship eventually resembles a parent-child or caregiver-patient relationship. Nonetheless, bodies are still warm and memories and images can be recalled or conjured. A great number of elderly without partners or with very ill partners report pleasure derived from fantasy and self-stimulation.

In addition, a number of elderly people told me that they derive tremendous sexual satisfaction with their partners from physical intimacies that do not include intercourse. Ken Kroll and Erica Levy Klein (1992), a disabled husband and his non-disabled wife, help to destroy the myth that only intercourse is "real sex" in an illuminating and tender book, *Enabling Romance*. In the book, people with a variety of physical limitations (e.g., spinal-cord injuries, amputations, neuromuscular disabilities, and spastic conditions) reveal that when illness or trauma took away sensation in areas generally regarded as "erogenous zones," other parts of their bodies became eroticized, capable of both giving and receiving sexual pleasure (often to orgasm). For example, when people's joints were painful or inflexible, they made their lovemaking leisurely and gentle and incorporated pillows and nontraditional positions, demonstrating that "where there's a will, there's a way" (Kroll & Klein, 1992, p. 42).

PART III

VALUES

CHAPTER 8

VALUES AND AGING

"We [the aged] may not be able to butter our bread, but we can still change the world."
—*Maggie Kuhn (1991, p. 15)*

Hubert and Beth are gone now. Hope, the country doctor, and Marianne, the matriarch of the beach-house, and many of the others I interviewed have also died. Shortly after completing the study, I moved to another state. My friend Elsa, who lives near Franklin Village, sends me newspaper clippings about the community, which keeps me informed about the birthdays, tributes, and passings of my old friends.

After my departure from Franklin Village, I did a *content analysis* that contributed to Chapters 2 through 7. Chapters 8, 9, and 10 will reflect on my experience as a participant-observer and will consider value orientations in late life and their implications for psychotherapy and *long-term care*.

PERSONAL REFLECTIONS

Early on, Hubert pointed out that "aspiration" was too lofty a word for older people. It was easier for older people to relate to words like *goals*, *dreams*, and *priorities*. In order for me to become part of the community, my words and phrases had to "fit" the age, culture, and life experiences of the residents at Franklin Village. For example, the residents were more relaxed and talkative when I identified myself as "a student learning about older people" instead of the more intimidating "a researcher studying aspirations." Being a "researcher" meant, at least to this population, that I might scrutinize and analyze everything they said or did. No one wants to feel as if he or she is living in a fishbowl.

On the second day of the study, I was put to the test. Beth invited me to breakfast with some of her friends. We had just been served our meals when a male resident turned to me and said, "I guess you're studying us." I said, "Please don't feel uncomfortable. I am not studying anything right now but my bacon." He laughed and said, "OK, I guess that means that you are 'off duty.'" (Actually, ethnographers are never off duty, but they should never appear to be "on duty.") Towards the end of the study, the same gentleman said, "I really like your technique. We were interviewed and we didn't even know it."

Rather than asking, "How old are you?" which elicited only a number (and once a mild rebuke for asking personal questions), I began to ask, "When were you born?" This question was received warmly. In addition to the age of the respondents, it frequently stimulated memories about growing up or recollections of world events that occurred before I was born.

I learned that subtle, sometimes unconscious motivations such as a researcher's desire to be "liked" influences the work. For example, because I feared that she would not like me, I lied to Hope, pretending to be happily married when I was actually separated. I mistook one participant's dignified and reserved regal bearing for an expression of her dislike for me, which short-circuited our relationship. And I declined an invitation to the Current Events Club merely because I was not "up" on the news; I feared that if my ignorance was discovered, I would not be respected or liked. After the initial days of the study, when it became apparent that I *was* liked, my concern diminished, and I was able to be myself.

It was disarming to realize that my presence changed the community that I tried so hard to capture "as is." Beth (as I had hoped) invited people to her apartment and to her breakfast table so that I would meet still more residents (an uncharacteristic behavior). Hubert transformed himself into a guide and mentor, perhaps fulfilling his need to nurture someone from the younger generation. It was no coincidence that the theme of a Sunday Quaker meeting "spontaneously" became *goals in late life*. And yet I am confident that the essence of Franklin Village was captured, tainted as it was by my presence.

The more involved with the community I became, the more frequently I experienced the emotion of surprise. Every time it occurred, I noted the circumstance (i.e., my thoughts, whom I was with, and what had transpired). When I reviewed my *field notes*, it became apparent that when reality did not conform to my beliefs about older people, I experienced surprise.

I began to use my emotional responses as tools (in addition to my cognitive skills) to understand the subjective world of the community as well as my biases. Whenever I met a resident with a strong, clear voice (and there were many), I was taken aback. Whenever I met a person who moved energetically, who got in and out of a chair quickly and easily, I felt unsettled. When Edith told me that she often stayed up all night to preserve the raspberries and cherries she grew, I thought, "An old woman should not stay up all night." I was taken aback when Hubert commented on a female resident's "nice legs." I was amazed when 97-year-old Simon told me about his trip to China three years earlier. My amazement was compounded when he told me that his son (who was 74) also went on the trip, which was organized for senior citizens. That older people had children who were also old, and that they might travel together, obviously did not fit with my image of older people. That an old man could admire the body of an old woman did not fit my belief system.

One event was particularly memorable. When Simon said that he would meet with me, providing that he didn't become confused and disoriented and wander about before the appointed time, I was again surprised. That an older person might be aware of his infirmities and discuss them so easily (and without embarrassment) at first made me uncomfortable. Then it seemed humorous. Why should I have believed otherwise? "Old" does not mean that one is unconscious about or insensitive to changes in one's phenomenology. I have since learned that when it comes to infirmities (their own and those of others), most older people are more tolerant than younger people. All this— from one so sensitive to ageism!

VALUE ORIENTATION

The explorations of aspirations and personal values reveal how older people experience their lives. Such an exploration helped me to get "inside aging" at Franklin Village in order to understand the experience of the people who live there. Possessing *values* or "conceptions of the desirable" (Kluckhohn, 1951, p. 395) is part of human nature.

Rokeach (1973), a major contributor to values research, divided values into two basic types: (1) *instrumental values*, which are specific ways of acting or being (modes of conduct), and (2) *terminal values*, which are specific ways of existing (end-states). For example, a *life of material wealth* would be a terminal value, whereas *being courageous* would be an instrumental value. Instrumental values can motivate behaviors that will help achieve the ideals of terminal values. Residents at Franklin Village hold both terminal values (e.g., a life filled with *pleasure*) and instrumental values (e.g., *helpfulness*).

Values have a *cognitive* component; in other words, people have an intellectual conception of what is the "right" way to behave or what are the "correct" goals to pursue. For instance, years of caring for their frail parents had a traumatic effect on Arthur and Edith's family life. They were emotionally and financially burdened by their caregiving responsibilities. Because of this experience, they especially valued *independence*. They reasoned that moving to Franklin Village was the logical thing to do to maintain their own independence and protect their children from the burden of their care, should they need it as they aged.

Values have an *emotional* component, which means that people tend to have intense feelings about them. Arthur and Edith were determined to make the move and were proud that they could afford it. They vehemently defended their decision, arguing against the protestations of their relatives and friends, who thought that the couple were too young and too healthy to move into an institutional setting.

Values also have a *behavioral* component. Motivated by their value for independence and autonomy, Arthur and Edith moved to Franklin Village without a qualm and have never regretted it.

In addition to motivating behavior, values act as a *standard* by which one can evaluate oneself—in the present as well as in the past. If people are not conducting themselves in a way that is congruent with their values, guilt is likely the result (Scott, 1965). This was exactly what happened when Hubert realized that he was not being his usual kind and helpful self. Relief came when he dined with three lonely male residents who never had any guests join their table.

Older adults who are engaged in *life review* cannot help but measure their past behavior and the way in which they met life's challenges and expectations against their personal framework of values. The outcome of this inner evaluation influences life satisfaction in the later years and has an impact on self-esteem.

Values and attitudes are related but different concepts. Rokeach (1968, 1973) states that a value refers to a single belief of a specific kind that transcends specific objects or situations. An attitude, on the other hand, refers to an organization of several beliefs centered around a specific object or situation. For example, *social ties* (the belief that maintaining intimate human contact with friends and family is desirable) was one of the five most frequently expressed values held by the residents at Franklin Village. One may hold that value but nevertheless avoid Uncle Fred at Thanksgiving dinner because his chatter is annoying. Because attitudes are specific to situations, they number in the thousands, whereas values number in the dozens (Rokeach, 1973). It can be argued that the total number of values corresponds to and is limited by the number of human needs. Freud (1922) proposed only two needs, Maslow (1970) five, and Murray (1938) twenty-eight. Rokeach (1973) proposed thirty-six values.

Once a value is learned, it gets integrated into a *prioritized* system of values (Rokeach, 1973). In other words, a person's values are rank-ordered. Although the type and number of values may stay the same throughout a lifetime, the order is always subject to change. Therefore, a value system is "stable enough to reflect the fact of sameness and continuity of a unique personality socialized within a given culture and society, yet unstable enough to permit rearrangements of value priorities as a result of changes in culture, society and personal experience" (Rokeach, 1973, p. 11).

These individual arrangements of values (*value orientations* or *value hierarchies*) account for the endless variations in people. The notion that an individual holds one value above another value is key to understanding differences in the decisions that people make, the actions they take, their personal philosophies, and their sense of well-being.

People are not always aware of their value hierarchies. Although I made no attempt to uncover residents' individual rank-ordering, one could assume that (within this group) *independence* would rank first or second. Many of the residents had moved hundreds of miles from their families and friends. Their move to the community entailed giving away or selling cherished possessions. They did it because, in their view, it relieved their children from any future "burden" and helped them to maintain their independence longer than any other option.

The notion that value priorities change is also key to understanding *value conflicts* or *value dilemmas*. During a period of transition, one is likely to experience feelings of uncertainty, anxiety, and guilt. An example would be the career-driven "workaholic" whose value orientation is characterized by productivity, status, and upward mobility. The value of *family* is often secondary to a couple—until a first child is born. In the subsequent months, the workaholic parent is conflicted and emotionally distraught. Will he or she maintain a work ethic and an 80-hour work week, or cut back and shift to a value orientation in which actively raising the child becomes paramount?

THE DEVELOPMENTAL IMPERATIVE

One of the major questions in values research is, What causes specific value orientations to emerge and change over time? The answer to this question may offer clues to a single theory of human behavior or to the resolution of some social problems. Undoubtedly, the answer to that question is complex and multifaceted.

The *developmental imperative* is the notion that the demands of human growth and development (i.e., the developmental tasks) play a major role in shaping value orientations.* When one is confronted with such a task, at any age, the value that is most relevant to the task at hand assumes priority and restructures the value hierarchy.

To illustrate, young children value *pleasure* and *being good*, but before these tots master some degree of *impulse control, pleasure* has primacy. Eventually, *being good* to win Mother's love and approval increases in importance relative to other values. School-age children confronted with the demands of learning and the desire for the regard of their schoolmates will value personal *achievement, skill,* or *possessions,* rearranging their values to reflect the tasks that face them.

Adolescents are faced with the tasks of building strong attach-

---

*Gender is another factor that may account for value difference between individuals. Men, particularly in mid-life, appear to place achievement very high on the value framework, whereas women tend to place a higher value on relationships (Lowenthal, Thurnher, & Chiriboga, 1975).

ments to friends and developing intimate peer relationships. In this case, values get rearranged accordingly so that *attractiveness* may emerge as a primary value. Not measuring up to the standard of appearance or having the correct clothing causes emotional pain. When adolescents reach adulthood, their value orientation shifts from one in which *attractiveness* dominates to one in which *family* and *success* (defined as status, productivity, or material reward) dominates.

In mid-life, that may change to an orientation in which *helping the younger generation* and social and civic concerns ascend. In later adulthood, there is often a change in orientation that gives less importance to "the values of youth," such as appearance and personal achievement, and more importance to the values that flourished at Franklin Village—*autonomy, personal growth, helping, social ties*, and *pleasure*.

THE SOCIOCULTURAL IMPERATIVE

Although the organizing of personal value orientations is influenced by the process of human development, the values that individuals learn, in the first place, are largely determined by the *social values** of the society in which the individual lives. This forms the *sociocultural imperative*. For example, individualism, ambition, and competitiveness are basic values of the American society, and hence are ingrained in the personal value hierarchies of most Americans. It is likely that if *conservation of resources* were a guiding principle in a particular community, it would also be valued by the individual members of the community. *Conservation* in a Native American youth, for instance, is a reflection of his or her community's values about nature.

Social values are not inconsequential. They shape the media and the entertainment industry. They contribute to the forma-

---

*These are values that are held *by* groups. This is not to be confused with an individual's personal values *for* society—such as political neutrality.

tion of national budgets. They define all of society's institutions and affect our attitudes and behavior toward subgroups within the population.

The same can be said for the significance of *culture* on the genesis of personal values. The United States is a country of cultural diversity that encompasses many ethnic, class, and racial subgroups. Each cultural group transmits its values, beliefs, and characteristic patterns of behavior to its young. Throughout life, the arrangement of these core values is influenced by developmental tasks that are relevant to the culture, as well as by commerce with the larger society and the degree of *acculturation* and *assimilation* to the dominant culture.

Several studies suggest that ethnicity provides a considerable resource that can be drawn on in old age (Cuellar, 1978; Myerhoff & Simić, 1978; Simić, 1978, 1987). Simić (1987) writes about elderly Serbian-Americans in Northern California, who—after a lifetime of fluctuation in ethnic affiliation, reaffirm their ethnicity in their later years. Their culturally rooted values become important again, motivating intense participation in Serbian churches and organizations. They observe ethnic holidays and traditions with other Serbs (young and old). Renewed ethnic involvement helps them meet the challenges of old age described by Peck (see Chapter 4) and provides a sense of continuity to their lives.

THE PHYSICAL IMPERATIVE

To survive, one must satisfy the *physiological imperative* of hunger, thirst, and safety. That means food, water, and protection from the elements and from victimization. Obviously, a child, adolescent, adult, or older person who is hungry and never sure that there will be food to eat (or who is afraid to leave the house because of street violence) is going to have a value orientation colored by these concerns. Higher needs or values cannot become a priority until basic ones are met.

Maslow (1954) writes:

For the basically deprived man the world is a dangerous place, a jungle, an enemy territory populated by (1) those whom he can dominate and (2) those who can dominate him. His value system is of necessity, like that of any jungle denizen, dominated and organized by lower needs, especially the creature needs and the safety needs. The basically satisfied person is in a different case. He can afford out of his abundance to take those needs and their satisfaction for granted and can devote himself to higher gratifications. This is to say that their value systems are different, in fact *must* be different. (p. 232)

Maslow (1968, 1970) viewed the physiological needs as developmental in nature. Only when physiological needs are satisfied will the next level, safety needs, emerge. A need tends to dominate until it is satisfied. If one is starving, the physiological needs dominate. If one is being physically abused, the safety needs dominate. When these two levels of needs are satisfied, love and respect from others is the dominant need. The need for self-actualization only emerges when the other four levels of need are satisfied (see Figure 8.1).

In this domain, memories may be long, especially when the deprivation has been chronic. Years after the physiological threat has been removed, people can fear and guard against its return. The acquisition of goods and money (to buy more goods) may reign above any other value and remain constant despite sociocultural or developmental imperatives.

THE "VALUE FRIENDLY" ENVIRONMENT

Problems emerge for the elderly (and anyone else, for that matter) when their personal value orientations do not match or do not appear to match those of the larger society or the particular

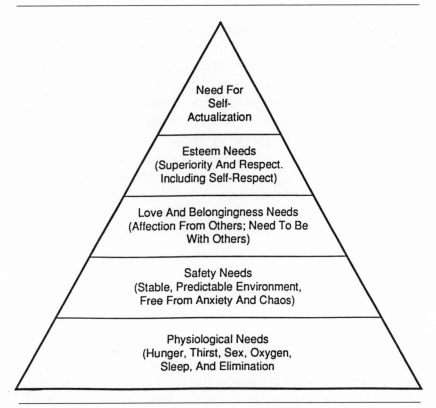

Figure 8-1. Maslow's need hierarchy. (Source: Maslow, 1968, 1970)

cultural environment in which they live. Such conflicts can seriously compromise the quality of life. For example, although the residents at Franklin Village demonstrate the contrary, most Americans view the elderly as passive, engaged in neither active mastery nor involvement with the external world. The aged are seen as past oriented and conservative "old fogies," as opposed to valued, future-oriented movers and shakers. "These apparent deviations by elders from the basic value orientations in our society tend to support prejudice and discrimination against them" (Palmore, 1990, p. 77).

Thomas and Chambers (1989) compared elderly men from two cultures with widely differing environments and value orientations—England and India. Their hypothesis was that *all* "adjusted" elderly share value orientations in which congeniality, cooperation, and relaxation are primary. Cultures in which these values dominate produce less stress for the aging person than cultures in which individualism, competition, and productivity dominate. In other words, some societies provide more satisfying environments for aging because their dominant value structures are congruent with the personal values of elderly persons and "friendlier" to the developmental tasks of old age.

Because Western measures of life satisfaction may not be appropriate for non-Western societies, the Thomas and Chambers study had some problems in measurement. Nevertheless, the researchers were able to conclude that the elderly Indian respondents had a greater acceptance of life and contentment than did their English counterparts. The Indian *culture* (which still retains a strong identification with cultural Hinduism) may be more amenable to the realities of dealing with the universal tasks of old age, particularly physical decline and proximity of death. It is a culture in which cooperation, not individualism, is the prevalent ideology. Unlike the English (and American) society, which dreads dependency and offers few roles for the elderly, the Indian society legitimizes dependency needs and supports continued involvement in religious practices and in the welfare of the family. For example, traditional Hindu law sets forth a four-stage life cycle for high-caste men (student, householder, ascetic, and mendicant). In the last two stages, elderly men are expected to renounce their worldly attachments to seek enlightenment in isolated retreats. Thus, these elderly have well-defined roles in their later years (Sokolovsky, 1983). Of course, India (and other non-Western societies) may only be "friendly" to the aging process if one is free from the ravages of poverty.

But what has all this to do with Franklin Village? Franklin Village offered Hubert, Beth, Hope, Annabelle, and the other residents an *environment* that was compatible with their values, a setting in which they could be free to pursue their aspirations.

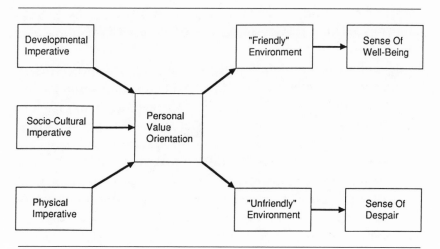

Figure 8-2. Value-friendly environments for the elderly.

Figure 8.2 depicts this process: Development (the challenges of old age), society, and physical needs form personal value orientations. When there is a "friendly" fit between the characteristics of the environment and those values, the outcome for the older adult is a sense of well-being. On the other hand, if the environment thwarts the expression of values and the pursuit of aspirations, the outcome is a sense of despair and a poor quality of life.

Lily, for example, wants only to be independent, to have her tea and ice cream whenever she likes. At Franklin Village, she will not have to relinquish her apartment for a room in the nursing facility until she requests it. Although the staff worries about her choice to remain in her apartment, which is certain to cause her some pain and suffering, they are committed to helping Lily remain autonomous. Everything is provided—nutritious meals, medical care, companionship when desired, telephone checks, a walker, and—above all—respect and patience. At 98, Lily is happy. She enjoys the privacy of her own apartment and the dear mementos it contains. Because she holds independence in such high regard, she holds *herself* in high regard for being able to maintain her autonomy in the face of old age and increasing disability. Imagine the quality of her life if she lived in a setting in which she had little privacy, where she was dressed by an aide and compelled to live by someone else's notion of when to eat or go to sleep.

The ethos of Franklin Village is also conducive to fulfilling altruistic desires that arise in old age. The Quaker residents are able to maintain their long traditions of helping. Both Quakers and non-Quakers find that—even at 95—it is easy to help a neighbor at Franklin Village. If the ladies want to knit sweaters and booties for third-world children, management supplies the yarn. When Sylvia wanted to teach itinerant farm workers how to read, management supplied her with transportation to the local high school. When Andrew wanted to collect newspapers and aluminum cans for recycling, management assisted with the heavy labor and transportation to the recycling center. When Beth and Cynthia wanted to clown, management provided them with space in the nursing home to store their makeup and change into their costumes.

Promoting helping behavior among the residents sometimes requires the staff to do less, not more. Residents are permitted to push the wheelchairs of their friends, even though it might be more expedient to have a stronger staff member to do it. Healthy husbands and wives are allowed to help feed and care for their ill or dying spouses in the nursing home. Residents who are interested are trained to "safely" guide wandering, confused, or demented residents back to the nursing home grounds. This is helpful to the entire community, since restraints are not used and a staff member might not be present.

Franklin Village has a value-friendly atmosphere. It imposes no institutional structure (i.e., no schedule of programs); rather, it supports and supplies resources for all community-initiated programs. The community is unique in that it has no Program Director to set up Bingo on Tuesday evenings, square-dancing on Fridays, and movies every other Thursday. The program committees are initiated by residents. Typically, someone gets an idea, finds other interested residents, and presents the idea to the administration, which usually responds with, "OK, what do you need?" If a group of women are interested in making jewelry, an instructor is procured and a room designated. If a group wants to start a model train club, the administration will offer its assistance. These environmental opportunities are congruent with the values of autonomy, pleasure, and personal growth.

The community fosters intimate social ties among residents and among staff and residents. Families visit often, sometimes staying overnight in the guest house. While I was there, I met a grandchild who was staying for several weeks to help Grandmom make the difficult transition from apartment to nursing home. Beth's daughter stayed the summer to visit Mom and to complete her social work internship in the community.

The notion that the well-being of the old is dependent on the fit between features of the environment and individual characteristics of the elderly was expressed in the *congruence model of person-environment fit* (French, Rodgers, & Cobb, 1974; Kahana, 1975) nearly 20 years ago. The origins of this theory are in Lewin's (1951) notion that behavior is a function of the relationship between the person and the environment.

It is also rooted in Murray's (1938) *need-press* model of behavior. In that model, environmental press is the counterpart to internalized needs. Environmental press may facilitate or thwart the gratification of needs. Indeed, people tend to seek settings that are congruent with their needs (presuming that they are aware of those needs). When there is dissonance between the press and the needs, the individual attempts to change the environment or to leave it. If change or relocation is not possible, the individual is forced to suffer the consequences of a poor fit. Adjustment, therefore, becomes defined as the "goodness of fit" (French, Rodgers, & Cobb, 1974, p. 316).

What I propose to add to the congruence paradigm is an emphasis on the fit between personal value orientations and environmental supports for the fulfillment of those values (and the aspirations they motivate). The next chapter will look at how this fit might impact psychotherapy with older adults.

CHAPTER 9

VALUES AND ASPIRATIONS REVISITED: IMPLICATIONS FOR PSYCHOTHERAPY

"I believe that man's noblest endowment is his capacity to change."
—*Leonard Bernstein (Cited in Kenworthy [1987], p. 33).*

Selma (see p. 3), a childless 68-year-old widow, is not doing well. Shortly after hearing that she had a "bad ticker" and needed bypass surgery, Selma began to despair about her "lonely life" and "poor health." Although her surgery was successful, she remains emotionally distressed. She spends her days watching television, taking medications for several chronic health problems, monitoring her bodily sensations, and worrying over every ache and pain. A good bit of her time is spent visiting doctors and seeking new medical specialists.

For 40 years, George (see p. 3), 77, and his wife, Mona, worked side by side in their women's apparel shop. Despite George's tendency towards pessimism and "gloom" (suffered since early childhood), life was satisfying. When Mona died three years ago, George's "normal" gloominess evolved into a severe depression. Finally, at the behest of his daughter, George agreed to move in with her family. Now his daughter has become frustrated with his unkempt appearance and all-day television watching, his teenage grandson has been arrested for shoplifting, and his son-in-law resents the time his wife spends on George's care.

Herman and Inez, married for 55 years, are miserable. Their marriage was always stormy, but no one had ever seemed concerned. Instead, their emotionality was accepted as "normal." Relatives comment, "Some people talk to each other; Herman and Inez scream at each other." However, to everyone's surprise, Inez is planning to leave Herman and move in with her divorced daughter.

If Freud were still alive, he would doubt the capacity of the individuals in these vignettes to benefit from "talking therapy." He wrote that older people were not educable, and thus they would make poor *analysands* (Freud, 1924). This belief was based on the assumption that personality is molded in childhood and that psychological symptoms are linked to childhood trauma. Therefore, old people (who have had decades of fixed traits) are unlikely to change. Despite research evidence to the contrary, some clinicians still believe that psychotherapy is not appropriate for the elderly.

Fortunately, most theorists (including psychoanalysts) tend to take a more expansive view of the dynamics of human behavior. They agree that symptoms can result from more recent experiences (e.g., loss, changing bodies, changing social roles, family chaos, poor skills, or the strain of inadequate resources and opportunities) as well as early childhood trauma. From this contemporary perspective, change is possible at any age if certain conditions for change are present.

Despite poor health, disabilities, relationship problems, or long standing emotional difficulties, individuals can make significant changes in their later years. Age is only one of several factors to consider when psychotherapy is indicated. It is not a measure of the worthiness of initiating a psychotherapeutic endeavor, nor is it an indication of prognosis.

However, age does require that the psychotherapist be familiar with the challenges inherent in this phase of life. The capacity to develop therapeutic relationships with a cohort who is likely to have minimal experience in discussing emotions or family matters and very different life experiences from one's own is equally important. The therapist may also have to discover ways to compensate for slower cognitive processing, visual and hearing losses, or fatigue in some of their frailer older clients. This chapter will highlight a number of issues related to psychotherapy with the older client, including the therapeutic usefulness of values and aspirations.

THE OLDER CLIENT

Jerome Cohen (personal communication, June 23, 1992) has outlined the client conditions that are necessary for effective psychotherapy with older adults. The older client must have:

- the capacity to learn, and to use that learning;
- the capacity to be creative (i.e., to "play with ideas," to dream, to fantasize, to anticipate, and to relate these images or thoughts to past, present, and future functioning). This includes the capacity to consider the development of new relationships and the redefinition of old ones (e.g., children, partners, siblings, parents);
- the capacity for self-observation in the present and the ability to reflect on the past (albeit with some tendency to erase some elements of the unpleasant);
- the capacity to be motivated to examine one's lifestyle and to reexamine goals and aspirations;
- the ability to re-experience the lingering feelings (often decades old) that inhibit growth and development (e.g., unresolved grief).

Cohen acknowledges that as long as there is a modicum of elasticity (i.e., the ability to accommodate to new ideas or situations), the older adult can benefit from psychotherapy, even when all of the above conditions are not met.

Although this chapter addresses psychotherapy with non-demented elderly, clients who are in the early stages of dementing illnesses such as Alzheimer's disease may also profit from psychotherapy. Approximately 25% of patients in the early stages of dementia experience depression as they become aware of their declining mental abilities (Hinrichsen, 1990). Psychotherapy can often reduce this depression and assist these clients in making realistic plans for the future.

THE PSYCHOTHERAPIST

I have found that the clinicians who genuinely like older people are the ones who are the most effective. For several years now, I have asked my gerontology students, "Why do you want to work with this population?" Without exception, every response has included a description of a meaningful personal relationship between the student and an elderly person. For example: "Mrs. Engle took care of me after my mother died. She was the only one who ever was able to make me feel safe." or "I volunteered in a nursing home when I was in junior high school. I'll never forget Mrs. Thomas." or "As a child, I shared my bedroom and my childhood secrets with my grandmother. She was my ally against our 'common enemy'—Mom and Dad."

Aging bodies, illness, grief, and dying are realities in psychotherapeutic work with older people. They are realities that most clinicians would rather circumvent because to do otherwise might mean that they would have to face their own aging and mortality. Having an early rewarding experience with an older person (such as the experiences mentioned above) tends to counter the common tendency to avoid issues of aging. Such experiences may also buffer the discomfort of discussing difficult material.

Unfortunately, when early impressions are negative, they may contribute to an unwillingness to engage older clients. Langer (1989) writes about the power of "premature cognitive commitments." These are early images in which meaning (rather than motion) is frozen. For example, if a child's early experiences with old age consist of contact with a disagreeable, cranky person with few redeeming qualities, the child is likely to form a premature conception of old age. That conception or premature cognitive commitment becomes a "snapshot" that is the foundation for everything learned about old age. The image is so ingrained that it may become difficult to change even in the face of contradictory information.

Besides a genuine affection for the elderly and a willingness to explore topics that most would rather avoid, psychotherapists may also have to adjust their interviewing styles to particular age-related impairments and cohort effects. The clinicians' guide (Table 9.1) offers "tips" to enhance the communication.

TABLE 9.1
The Clinician's Guide to Interviewing Elderly Clients

General Strategies
- Older clients tend to conceptualize problems as either physical (e.g., "masked depression") or moral (e.g., the result of sin). It is helpful to explain the usefulness of *talking* about problems, expressing feelings, and gaining understanding.
- The use of touch to communicate caring and interest is especially important with older people. More often than not, older people are not hugged or touched because of limited social contacts or ageism.
- Silence during an interview can mean many things (anxiety, anger, nothing to say, quiet reflection, etc.). With older people, it may also be a result of a physical process (e.g., aphasia, slower processing due to aging or impairment, confusion, memory loss). Mentioning the silence in a neutral manner (e.g., "sometimes it is hard to talk") is often sufficient to move the client. Better yet, allow the client the freedom to be silent.
- Elderly people are at high risk for alcohol abuse. It is therefore important to overcome a natural reticence in asking older people about their drinking habits.
- The biggest fear of many elderly people is institutionalization. This fear may make them reluctant to discuss their problems. The way to diminish their fear is to clearly state the goal of the interview.

- Elderly suicide rates are higher than in the general population (especially for white males). Because the elderly tend to talk less about suicidal intentions and make fewer "manipulative" gestures, clinicians need to be particularly thorough in assessing suicide risk.

Impairments and Diminishments

- If the client does not hear a phrase, do not repeat it over and over again. Some sounds are more difficult to hear than others, so paraphrasing is more useful than repetition.
- Be careful not to lower the volume of your voice when discussing sensitive topics (sexuality, alcohol, suicide).
- Avoid speaking in a high-pitched voice, which is harder to hear than a low-pitched voice.
- Speak as clearly as possible. Make sure your face is in the light to help facilitate lip-reading.
- Because hearing aids magnify extraneous sounds, eliminate TV noises, nearby conversations, and the like.
- If you suspect mild dementia, avoid scheduling evening interviews, when "sundowning" (confusion at nightfall) is likely to occur.
- Although older people do not generally show a noticeable decline in intellectual functioning, they may take longer to respond to questions. They may also be overly cautious to avoid making errors. Therefore, allow more time for an interview. The elderly need 15% more time to respond.
- Older people do not have great energy reserves and may tire faster than younger clients. Watch for nonverbal signs of fatigue, which might make their responses less accurate. When this happens, it is better to schedule another interview.

Cohort Effects

- Older people grew up in a time when "personal problems" were not discussed. You will have to allow extra time for them to feel comfortable about discussing these matters.
- Older people grew up in a period when elders were called by surnames. Most older clients will prefer being addressed as "Mr. Smith," "Mrs. Jones," or "Miss Brown" instead of as "John" or "Mary."

Family

- Interview elderly clients alone, unless their memories are so poor that friends or relatives must be present to supply necessary information. Remember that, just as with other clients, it may be easier for them to talk about personal problems when alone. We want to avoid the suggestion that elderly people are unable to present their situations because of their age.
- Sometimes older people will present the problem that they think will be

more interesting to the professional or that their children feel is most
important. Therefore, it is necessary to ask, "What problem is most
strongly interfering with your life?" (Brummel-Smith, 1986).

Transference, Countertransference
- Be aware of transference phenomena with elderly clients who may relate
  to you as if you were their child, grandchild, or parent.
- Be aware of countertransference with elderly clients. It is especially common to relate to an elderly client in a way in which you might relate
  to your parent or grandparent.

PSYCHOTHERAPY WITH OLDER ADULTS

Earlier, I wrote that age is neither a measure of the worthiness
of initiating a psychotherapeutic endeavor nor an indication of
prognosis. However, age does appear to make a difference in the
epidemiology of mental disorders. People with schizophrenia, for
instance, usually become ill early in life. They have higher rates
of suicide and traumatic death than people without this disorder,
making it rare for a person with this condition to survive to old
age (Gurland & Cross, 1982).* In contrast, there are higher rates
of dementia among the old, especially among those who live in
institutional settings. *Mental Health Problems and Older Adults*
(Hinrichsen, 1990) is an excellent starting point for reading
about the psychotherapeutic treatment and management of
organically brain-impaired and psychotic elderly.

During the rest of this chapter, however, I shall address psychotherapy with older adults whose emotional distress is frequently related to illness, grief, and dying and the challenge of
maintaining a life that is congruent with personal values and
aspirations.

Psychotherapy texts written with a *diagnostic approach* provide
instruction for alleviating or "curing" particular symptoms or
syndromes (Turner, 1992). Texts written with a *method approach*
(e.g., Dorfman, 1988) describe theoretical orientations and tech-

---

*Schizophrenia is found in approximately 1% of those over 65 (Babigian & Lehman, 1987).

niques. Finally, a third way of addressing the material is a *client approach*, which emphasizes the clinical issues that arise in working with particular populations, such as children, people with AIDS, or African Americans. I have taken the last approach, highlighting some of the clinical issues that emerge when conducting psychotherapy with older adults.

Transference and Countertransference

Having a generally warm regard for old people and being able to listen (really listen) and communicate (adjusting for age-related needs) are essential ingredients of psychotherapy practice with this population. Understanding the aging experience (as well as one is able), being familiar with resources, and having the capacity to elicit and "stay with" difficult material despite the natural inclination to switch to more "pleasant" subjects are additional ingredients.

Still another component of effective clinical work with the aged is the awareness of the way in which clients and therapists react to each other. Such reactions may have little to do with reality and may interfere with the treatment process. These reactions are called *transference* and *countertransference*.

Transference is a term that is used to describe a phenomenon that is common to all human relationships. People frequently have feelings and attitudes about other people that do not fit the characteristics of those individuals or the reality of the present situation. The feelings are instead merely repetitions of early feelings toward significant persons from childhood, usually (but not always) parents. Transference can be observed in everyday life in nonclinical situations. For example, an individual who meets every employer, teacher, or doctor with hostility might be transferring to current authority figures old feelings that originally were directed toward an abusive father.

In classical psychoanalysis, these reactions are central to treatment. The analyst encourages the development of transference by becoming a "blank screen" and cautiously withholding opinions or personal information from the client, who lies on a couch, unable to see the analyst's face. These and other methods foster *regression* and stimulate transference. In psychoanalysis, the transference distortions are interpreted to the client, with the intent of resolving the client's unconscious conflicts. In other psychotherapeutic orientations, interpretation may or may not be shared with the client. Nevertheless, the therapist's understanding of the transference helps him or her to illuminate clients' past and present functioning.

Handling transference phenomena with older clients is particularly complex. For instance, the therapist is usually younger than the client. This means that the older client may act as though the therapist is not only a parent but also a child or grandchild. If clients experience therapists as children, they may expect that care will be provided in the form and manner of "dutiful" offspring. Some older clients idealize their therapists, bragging to friends about their accomplishments or intelligence in the same way they would boast about a grandchild. Clients may also re-create archaic parent-child power struggles.

Countertransference (a concept that also originated in classical psychoanalysis) refers to an intense reaction toward a client that stems from the *therapist's* own unconscious conflicts. If these reactions (and their origins) remain out of the therapist's awareness, they may interfere with the therapeutic process and may actually be harmful to the client.

In contemporary psychotherapy practice, countertransference has come to have a much broader meaning. It includes the *totality* of unconscious and conscious feelings experienced by therapists toward their clients, including those feelings evoked by the client's behavior or by current and past events in the therapist's life (Katz, 1990). No longer is it considered strictly a destructive phenomenon to identify and overcome. Instead, countertransference responses, when recognized, are used as tools to illuminate "blind spots" and to propel the clinician on a course of self-exploration and increased competency.

This is especially true when working with older clients. Consider Selma. A therapist might lecture her about how she needs to get out and meet people, volunteer, and develop hobbies. Selma may pay little heed to bright optimism about what she might still accomplish. The therapist might then feel increasingly helpless and frustrated—even angry—with her as the months pass and, despite great therapeutic efforts, her world grows ever more narrow and organized around her ill and aging body.

If challenged by a colleague to examine his or her countertransference reactions, Selma's therapist might come to realize that those reactions emerged from personal anxiety about aging and loneliness. In this case, the therapist made a common error. Instead of trying to understand "where Selma is," which might require allowing her to grieve for her losses and discuss the proximity of death, the therapist tried to get Selma to join in avoiding the whole issue.

Working with older people can also rekindle feelings and old issues that one has had with one's own parents. For example, therapists who find themselves excessively explaining their own behavior, self-disclosing more than usual, or becoming hurt when an older client questions their expertise, may be reacting to the client as if the client were a parent.

Sometimes, of course, countertransference feelings do not arise from the therapist's unconscious, but are empathic responses to a client's emotional state. The sorrow a therapist might experience when working with Selma could be a manifestation of his or her capacity to empathize with Selma's sadness as she relates the atrocities she endured in a Nazi death camp and as she talks about the death of her little brother, the loss of every member of her extended family, an unrequited love, and the children she never had.

Countertransference can thus be useful to the development of rapport between client and clinician. When my students pair their interest in gerontology with fond memories of old people, we can predict that many of their kind and loving reactions to their older clients will be rooted in their early relationships with particular older adults.

Family and Couple Issues

Some elderly people outlive all of their relatives. Others are abandoned by or estranged from the ones who are alive. Nevertheless, it is incorrect to assume that all elderly are in this situation. On the contrary, evidence shows that the majority of older people have strong family ties and that most elder-care is provided by family members (Moroney, 1980). As the number of older people increases, and four- and five-generation families become commonplace, family relations will assume even greater importance.

Since the late 1940s and early 1950s, many psychotherapists have been conceptualizing "individual" symptoms as family problems. In this approach, the family system is the vehicle for understanding how symptoms and problems are created, maintained, and "cured." Until recently,* most family treatment was focused on the problems of childhood and adolescence, and the old folks were simply left out. Older adults were not recognized as part of their families' problems, nor were they recognized as part of the families' solutions.

Families often have trouble adjusting to transitions and role changes. Family members become disorganized, confused, or overwhelmed; secrets are kept (at great cost); offspring repeat the behavior patterns of their parents and grandparents. Vulnerable family members become scapegoats or "black sheep," enabling others to avoid the "real" issues. People forget (or never learned how) to communicate their feelings to each other.

The case of George offers an example of the kinds of issues that can emerge within families of the elderly. Having an emotionally distressed grandfather move into the family home upset the *equilibrium* of the system. The daughter became preoccupied

---

*Neidhardt and Allen (1993) have written an excellent text describing family therapy with the elderly.

with her father's care, her husband became resentful, the grandson (perhaps reacting to the tension between his parents, as well as to the loss of former parenting) became a shoplifter. Old conflicts might have been rekindled. The family did not have the flexibility and resources to accommodate to the changes in a healthy way.

In family treatment, family members are encouraged to express their feelings, voice their concerns and expectations, and air their grievances. Members of the older generation can be invaluable in family work. They are often the first to reveal "secrets," which then gives the rest of the family permission to do the same without feeling disloyal. When old people talk about their adult children, it helps the youngest to view their parents differently. It is very likely that neither George nor the others have adequately mourned the loss of Mona—a situation that can be contributing to the problems within the family.

As Art Linkletter (1985) has written, "Old age is not for sissies." Growing old means confronting and adapting to a variety of demanding challenges and experiences, including retirement, "empty nests," the children's sometimes unfortunate return to the nest, housing changes, disability, and changes in health, appearance, and functioning. Some older people seem to sail effortlessly through these tasks, while others suffer considerable emotional and physical pain. Most are somewhere in between. In the best circumstances, partners help and support each other, each taking on new roles or modifying others when necessary. However, that is not always the case. It is not uncommon for partners to differ in their coping strategies. Herman and Inez demonstrate the way in which a coping mechanism that might be effective for one partner is disastrous for the couple's relationship.

The death of Inez's 95-year-old mother propelled Inez and Herman into the realization that they were in the final stages of their own lives. "Liberated" from caring for her mother, Inez turned her attention to her divorced daughter and grandchild. In other words, she coped with the loss of her mother and her own fear of aging by focusing on the activities and company of youth.

Herman, on the other hand, did not have a coping strategy and thus became obsessed with his diminished abilities and regrets. He reacted to Inez's "abandonment" with ill temper and mean-spiritedness. Neither Herman nor Inez realized that they were struggling, each in their own way, with their fears about dependency, mortality, loss of roles, and changing lifestyle. Their combative communication style only hindered mutual empathic understanding and exacerbated their problems.

Couples who never resolved long-standing conflicts (e.g., about roles and expectations, the balance of power, finances, and sex) during their work and child-rearing years may experience an escalation of these long-standing conflicts in late life. Wolinsky (1990) has written a book that specifically addresses the long-standing conflicts and the developmental issues faced by older couples, as well as the role that these issues play in the *etiology* and treatment of problems among older couples.

Loss and Grief

The emotional distress and the dilemmas that accompany loss can be thrust upon older adults in a single shocking moment (e.g., after the unanticipated death of a partner) or can emerge gradually with the passage of time (e.g., with the decline in energy, the deterioration of one's own health or one's partner's health, or changes in social and family roles). Although loss is not exclusive to old age, most people would agree that it is certainly a predominant theme. Grieving for, adapting to, and recovering from the losses inherent in this phase of life is one of the most compelling tasks—if not the major challenge—of late life.

People's ability to cope varies. Most older adults eventually integrate their losses into their self-image. They may accommodate with a sense of humor or quiet acceptance, but usually in a way that is consistent with the coping styles that they have practiced for decades.

Coping strategies can be effective, or they can be destructive—

for instance, abuse of over-the-counter medication or alcoholism. A common coping strategy is to use *suppression* (i.e., not permitting oneself to feel unpleasant emotions).

There are people who *never* (or hardly ever) allow themselves to experience the sadness, guilt, anger, and hurt that accompanies loss. Over time, most of their available energy is used to block those feelings from consciousness. Regrettably, the consequence is costly. Vital energy is less available for living fully. The person is only "half alive"—isolated, fatigued, helpless, and hopeless— chronically depressed. Clinicians working with such clients must assist them in unraveling years of accumulated loss and help them endure the consequent psychic pain that surfaces. Such clients must repeat the story of their losses and re-experience the emotions before their energy is released for pleasurable pastimes. Novice therapists frequently grow impatient and report to their supervisors, "I am getting nowhere; we simply go over and over the same material." For some, the process is brief; for others, lengthy. It is as if there is a "magic number"—that is, the client must go through the process an unknown number of times before the mourning is complete.* Selma, for instance, may have never fully mourned earlier losses. Her situation illustrates the way suppressed mourning can lead to chronic depression, which may include hypochondriasis†.

Suppression of the emotions that accompany loss may be played out in quite another way, albeit with an apparently more satisfactory outcome. Witness the recent widower who behaves in the opposite way from what one might expect. Instead of grieving, he exhibits an immediate zest for activities, becomes adventuresome, and may make rash decisions—including

---

*The notion of *accumulated loss* helps us to understand cases in which someone *decompensates* to suicidal proportions over what looks, at first glance, to be a relatively minor loss. Exploration often uncovers a lifetime of unmourned losses at the root of the person's current emotional state and behavior.

†Hypochondriasis offers a way for some individuals to hold on to a measure of self-esteem while absolving themselves of responsibility for their problems (e.g., "It is not my fault. It is my body that has betrayed me.").

remarriage and pleasing himself with expensive trips and adult "toys." It is difficult to explain this behavior in light of the previous example. Perhaps, in this case, the grieving took place prior to the actual loss; or suppression works here in a way that does not rob energy. There is also the possibility that the grief is delayed and will arrive later like a ton of bricks. I have known situations where this "merry widow phenomenon" occurred with no serious consequences other than some hurt adult children who could not fathom how their father could have such a good time so quickly after the loss of his wife of 50 years.

Reminiscence

Memory is highly functional. The ability to recall, reflect on, and re-experience the past within the mind's eye enhances life (see pp. 14-15). Memories help us learn from the past. They are also the means by which we may pleasantly pass time or distract ourselves from current uncertainties and anxieties.

Reminiscence may serve even greater adaptive functions for the elderly. For example, when self-esteem is low due to physical or mental decline, how glorious it is to recall one's former greatness. When one's life is unsatisfying because of the loss of certain roles, how comforting it is to blame modern society and idealize the ways of the past. When death is imminent, how sweet it is to be able to reach back into the past—like Little Jack Horner reaching into the pie—pull out a "plum" of a memory, and say "What a good boy was I," reconstructing and reinterpreting events in order to form them into a more acceptable perspective. When one's opportunities for affecting the present seem nil, how gratifying it is to recall an anecdote from which young listeners can learn.

Reminiscence among the old is commonplace, perhaps even universal (Butler, 1963). Many psychotherapists capitalize on this spontaneous phenomenon by initiating a "Life Review" with their elderly clients. Techniques to stimulate memory include perusing memorabilia and photographs, encouraging the taping or writing of autobiographies, and constructing genealogies (Lewis & Butler, 1974).

However, Life Review is not an appropriate therapeutic strategy for all elderly clients. For some, the process rekindles old pain, guilt, and regrets that cannot be successfully *reframed* and reintegrated into a more satisfying life story. There are clients who call on the past to justify their assertion that they are unworthy and that their life has been useless. In these cases, the Life Review method is best dropped or never initiated.

Another form of Life Review is the Marital Review or Couple Review. Inez and Herman, for example, might strengthen their marital bond by recalling the many phases of their long marriage. They might be assisted in "stepping back" to view their current difficulties in the context of the 55-year span during which they overcame many problems. In such an enterprise, couples renew shared accomplishments and interdependence. The clinician guides them in recalling *their* former greatness by reconnecting them with their most positive individual and couple self-images. Alas, here too reminiscence is no panacea. If the couple persist in perceiving their marriage or partnership as a total failure, the review will only justify that end.

VALUE-ORIENTED PSYCHOTHERAPY

I did not start out on my first day at Franklin Village, nor in the early months of writing this book, with the intentions of developing a perspective on clinical work with the elderly. My goals were to try to understand the inner experience of aging and to simply communicate what I had learned. Nevertheless, as time passed and I reflected on the lives of the residents, I developed a substantial respect for the values and aspirations of the residents and the implications of those ideas for a value-oriented psychotherapy.

Psychotherapists who work with older clients have a smorgasbord of psychotherapeutic *paradigms* from which to select. The

major organizing principle of many of these therapeutic paradigms is the configuration of clients—for example, the individual,
the family, or the group. Psychotherapy models are also organized
by assumptions about theories of human behavior. For example,
psychoanalysis views behavior as motivated by unconscious drives
and defenses, whereas behavioral therapy views behavior in terms
of *learning theory*. Each model is shaped by the climate of the times
from which it originated and the observations and insights of its
founders. Explanations of problems, methods of assessment, and
techniques to attain therapeutic goals are specific to each psychotherapy paradigm (Dorfman, 1988).

What I have termed "Value-Oriented Psychotherapy" is not a
therapeutic paradigm. Rather, it is a *metaparadigm*, which means
that although it carries a set of assumptions about human problems and has particular therapeutic goals, it does not offer specific techniques. Instead, it provides a framework from which
specific techniques can be created.

Value-Oriented Psychotherapy requires that the therapist
approach the older client from a Janus-like position,* viewing
the client's past and future at the same time. In other words, the
clinician explores the client's aspirations and the values from
which those aspirations have sprung.

This approach rests on two assumptions. The first one is that
the despair (manifested in poor self-esteem, bitterness, self-
absorption, paranoia, hypochondriasis, interpersonal difficulties,
etc.) is, in part, the result of living incongruently with one's
values. The second assumption is that the uncovering of earlier
values and the restoration of a means of expressing them will
enhance the well-being of many older adults.

As we have seen, the realities of age challenge the capacity to
continue living in congruence with one's values. Many elderly
make these adaptations unconsciously. An excellent example of
such adjustment is illustrated by an older woman who donated

---

*The Roman god Janus, the patron saint of beginnings and endings, looked in two opposing direc-
tions at the same time.

her handiwork to the poor. Forty years of donations included richly embroidered Christmas tablecloths, tiny socks and mittens with whimsical figures, bed jackets with handmade appliqués, and beaded sweaters with matching hats. Her work was extraordinary, the kind of things sold in expensive boutiques or handed down as heirlooms. When friends asked why she made such fine items when it would be less costly, more practical, and easier to knit the usual sturdy woolens, she answered, "Because it is the right thing to do."

Her gifts demonstrated a long-held altruistic value—that one should regard the less fortunate in the same way one regards a beloved friend. So, when failing eyesight made the intricate work too difficult and a fixed income made it impossible to purchase expensive materials, she found a creative solution. Using remnants of yarn from decades of knitting, extra-large needles, and a simple stitch, she knitted shawls (with unusually striking combinations of color and texture) to warm the shoulders of people with AIDS.

Another more celebrated example can be found in the life of French artist Henri Matisse. In his final years, Matisse suffered from the effects of an intestinal disease. His abdominal wall was so damaged that he was never again able to stand upright for more than a few minutes at a time (Russell et al., 1969). When he became too frail to paint, Matisse's assistants "pushed" precolored paper "through" his scissors, enabling him to create astonishingly spirited cutouts that he then arranged into elaborate designs.

The acceptance of a cane when walking at twilight, the installation of handrails in the shower, or the request for a partner to ride "co-pilot" (as a second set of eyes) for an elderly driver are all manifestations of independence and autonomy values.*

---

*Adler attributed all *neurotic behavior* to inferiority feelings and consequent attempts to achieve superiority. He acknowledged that loss made the elderly particularly vulnerable to inferiority feelings. The usual methods of compensating—friendship, family, and career—are all reduced in the later years. Thus, older people may compensate in less healthy ways. *Organ dialect*, for instance, is an unconscious process in which people attempt to "speak" (Brink, 1979, p. 275) against their feelings of inferiority through organ disability. That is, they use their disabilities to obtain increased attention

In the case of Selma, death and ill health robbed her of the opportunity to express caring for her husband and her home. She redirected her "caring" inward with little satisfaction and much fear. A value-oriented assessment might begin to unearth and clarify her personal values with the following questions: What do you do in an average day? What would you like to be doing? What was a good day like for you at age 65? At 50? At 30? At 21? What kinds of things did people say about you (at 21, 30, 50, 65) that made you feel good? What made you feel bad? What is important in your life? When did these things become important to you? Did they continue to be important over the years? How did they change? When did you realize that? Who do you admire? Why? What are their personal qualities? What did you learn as a child about what is worthwhile in life or how people should be? What did you learn in adulthood about a worthwhile life or how people should be? What do you want to do with the rest of your life? What are your goals? Responses to these and similar questions assist older clients in understanding the connection between their sense of well-being and their personal values.

Selma's treatment would then proceed to an active problem-solving phase in which she and her therapist would consider things she might do to reestablish her connection with forgotten or lost values and aspirations. The therapist is a coach, an advocate, and a source of information about resources in the community that might assist—or, in Selma's case, be assisted by—the client's aspirations.

The next chapter will look at various types of environments for the elderly, with an eye toward "goodness of fit" between values and setting.

---

from others. Another method is *masculine protest*, in which the person attempts to recapture feelings of superiority by clinging to the vestiges of masculinity. In this situation, the individual may use combativeness or aggressive sexuality to attempt to master the environment (Brink, 1979).

CHAPTER 10

VALUE-FRIENDLY LONG-TERM CARE

"The organism tells us what it needs (and therefore what it values) by sickening when deprived of these values."
—*Abraham Maslow (1954, pp. 153–154)*

Residents of Franklin Village are indeed fortunate to grow old under *ideal* circumstances. Their environment supplies basic needs, fosters autonomy, supports personal growth, and is virtually free from the effects of ageism. Poverty, isolation, and inaccessibility to health care—factors that affect the well-being and stifle the potential of many older adults—are absent from their lives. Most importantly, they feel good about themselves because their life-styles are congruent with their personal values.

However, even Utopia cannot protect one from worn-out organs, hearing loss, and *Alzheimer's disease*. It is a fact of life that if one lives long enough, one will probably have to rely on others for help with *activities of daily living (ADLs)** and *instrumental activities of daily living (IADLs)*[†].

---

*ADLs (Katz, Downs, Cash, & Grotz, 1970; Katz, Ford, Moskowitz, Jackson, & Jaffe, 1963) include eating, toileting, dressing, bathing, and locomotion.

[†]IADLs (Lawton & Brody, 1969) include cooking, cleaning, doing laundry, handling household maintenance, transporting oneself, reading, writing, managing money, using the telephone, and comprehending and following instructions.

LONG-TERM CARE

The myriad of health, personal care, and social services for older adults (provided informally by families and formally by organizations and institutions) comprise what is known as *long-term care*. Long-term care usually begins with functional impairment. For example, following a stroke, Mom can no longer bathe or cook meals by herself. If there is an adult child, a sibling, or kindly neighbor who is willing to help (and the older person is willing to accept help), these needs will be met.

It is estimated that 73% of the care provided to the elderly comes from relatives, friends, or neighbors (Soldo & Manton, 1985). Not infrequently, however, relatives or friends are unable to help—or there are no friends or relatives to help. In those cases, assistance is often provided by formal services such as *Meals on Wheels* and paid homemakers or health aides. Formal services may come in a variety of arrangements and settings.

Community-based Services

Numerous community services have evolved to maintain (or improve) the functioning of the elderly within their own homes and neighborhoods, thereby avoiding more restrictive institutional living arrangements. *The Older Americans Act* (OAA), passed by Congress in 1965 and amended several times since, set up a network of state *Area Agencies on Aging* (AAA) that has been the impetus for the development of community services. These programs include information and referral services, counseling, education, recreation, transportation, protective services, homemaker services, day care, nutrition programs (hot meals served at congregate sites or delivered to homes), legal services, respite care, and senior centers.

Similar services are provided for low-income elderly by the *Social Service Block Grants Program*, a federal program established under Title XX of the *Social Security Act* (also in 1965). The services available through these two legislative acts vary widely from community to community.

Home Care

Despite increasing difficulty in accomplishing everyday tasks, most elderly will agree that "there is no place like home." A random-sample survey of more than 1,500 people 55 and over conducted by the American Association of Retired Persons found that the overwhelming majority (86%) of its members desire to stay in their homes indefinitely (AARP, 1990).

The only common denominator for elderly recipients of home care is that they dwell in home settings. That might be the house they lived in for decades, the apartment they retired to with their spouse, a room in their adult child's home, or a couple of rooms in a *retirement hotel*. Beyond that single common thread, home care is extremely diverse.

The rationale for home care (which encompasses both health and social services) is that it will postpone or prevent institutionalization. Also (if the cost of the housing is disregarded), home care services are likely to be less expensive than nursing home care. Nevertheless, it is no simple matter to organize and deliver the services required to prolong independent living. Maintaining "independence" may require the services of physicians, nurses, social workers, nutritionists, speech therapists, and physical and occupational therapists. It may also include home health aides (for personal care), homemaking services such as cleaning and cooking, paid companions, and even financial managers.

There must be an initial assessment to determine the appropriate services. Then these services must be contracted, coordinated, monitored, and paid for (publicly or privately). Older adults may need assistance in overcoming resistances to accepting help. Barriers to acceptance may be caused by cultural beliefs and feelings of pride, guilt, shame, or denial of impairment. Services may need to be increased as the person becomes more frail, or decreased as the family assumes more responsibility or the older person regains some functioning. Geriatric case management (also called care management) has emerged as a new professional role to fulfill these responsibilities.

Adult day care

When we think of *day care*, we are likely to envision small children going willingly or unwillingly into the care of others while parents go to work, conduct other important business, or rest. The tots play, eat a nutritious meal, learn to get along with other children, and bring home art projects that obviously have had generous adult input. If things go well, they learn to put on their jackets and pour milk. The hope is that the kids will benefit from intellectual stimulation and social interaction, but most of all that they will be protected from harm while their parents are away.

Adult day care shares many of these features, with the addition, in some situations, of medical, psychiatric, or rehabilitative services. Providers may include hospitals, nursing homes, social service agencies, churches, and free-standing enterprises. A great majority of the clients suffer from dementia. In that situation adult day care provides caregivers with several hours of respite in which they can rest, visit friends, or do chores. Although in theory it might allow a caregiver to maintain a job, in practice it rarely does. Clients usually attend only two or three days a week, and the day usually ends too early to permit the caregiver to retain a job with typical 9-to-5 hours.

Institutional Settings

Board and Care

There are a number of long-term care arrangements that are clearly not nursing homes but are institutional in the sense that the elderly person relocates from his or her own home to a new home that is shared by other people with varying degrees of mental or physical impairments. These *board and care homes* typically provide meals, a room, help with ADLs and IADLs, and 24-hour protection. Although they are nonmedical, usually the overseers can get prescriptions filled, supervise medications, and link residents with community services. They are typically family-owned and operated. This is not an arrangement for the elderly person who wanders, who is combative, or who needs close monitoring.

There are about 30,000 board and care homes in the United States, ranging from 1 to 500 beds, with an average of 14 beds per home. About half of the estimated 370,000 board and care residents are over 65 years old (Reichstein & Bergofsky, 1983).

Nursing Homes

Unlike the long-term care discussed above, nursing home care represents *total* institutionalization. (Although residents of some nursing homes are recipients of community services, most are not.) The nursing home is a setting in which medical and social services are provided, but most residents view it simply as the place where they live (Kane & Kane, 1987). There are more than 19,000 nursing homes in the United States (American Association of Homes for the Aging, personal communication, 1992).

And who lives there? Approximately 1.3 million moderately and severely disabled people reside in skilled and intermediate nursing facilities (National Center for Health Statistics, 1987).* Many factors make an elderly person more likely to be placed in a nursing home—for example, advanced age (85 or older), a recent hospital admission, impairment in ADLs, dementia, and multiple chronic illnesses. The factor that distinguishes most nursing home residents from equally impaired elders who continue to live in the community is the absence of a caregiver or

---

*The proportion of elderly who are institutionalized is less than 5%.

social support network. It has been shown that 25% of nursing home placements were precipitated by the illness or death of the caregiver (Colerick & George, 1986; Morycz, 1985).

Anyone who reads the newspaper or watches television newscasts is aware of the abuses and violations of regulations that can take place in these facilities. These sensationalized reports, although repugnant, do not represent the nursing care industry. Nevertheless, they perpetuate the common lament, "I'd rather die than go to one of those places." Actually, there are many excellent (although costly) nursing homes.

Cost is becoming an increasingly important concern as both young and old realize that an aging population will cause greater demands on society for financing long-term care. The average cost of care in a nursing home (depending on level of care required) is $20,000 to $25,000 a year; costs are as high as $50,000 a year in some parts of the country (AARP, 1991).

Most elderly cannot afford this kind of outlay—at least, not for very long. Those with incomes below a specified level (which varies across states) are eligible for *Medicaid*, which will reimburse certified nursing homes. Those who are not eligible have to *spend down* their assets—that is, pay their nursing home bills by depleting their assets and life savings in order to qualify for Medicaid. Watching life savings disappear in a matter of months and going on a welfare program designed for the poor is distressing to proud elderly people who have worked hard all their lives and who hoped to leave something behind for their children. For this and other reasons, there is movement afoot to establish a national health insurance program (including long-term care benefits) for all Americans.

Continuing Care Retirement Communities

Franklin Village is an example of one of the 800 life care or continuing care retirement communities (CCRCs) in the United States (American Association of Homes for the Aging, personal communication, 1992). The CCRC is a long-term housing option that includes comprehensive services.* Most residents regard the CCRC as a kind of lifetime social and health insurance plan (Williams, 1985). For a prepayment (usually a substantial entrance fee and/or monthly fees), a relatively healthy single person or a couple (in most cases, at least one partner must be 65 or over) is provided with an independent apartment, cottage, or house, and is guaranteed a full range of health care and social services on the premises for life. The majority of CCRCs (95%–98%) are owned and managed by not-for-profit organizations (Somers & Spears, 1992).

A CCRC is a *multilevel facility*—that is, there are several levels of care within the community so that services match all needs. For many couples, the most attractive advantage is that if one partner becomes seriously debilitated, the couple need not separate. The wife, for example, can retain her independent apartment and still spend her days with her husband, either in the nursing facility on the grounds or in their apartment. The fees do not increase as needs escalate. Residents who may require costly medical treatment and 24-hour skilled nursing care pay no more than when they required simple maintenance services for their apartments, meals, and routine medical check-ups.

It is interesting to note that studies show that life expectancy among residents of CCRCs is 20% longer than for the general population (Winklevoss, 1985). Another interesting finding is that in communities where there is free access to health care, health care utilization is lower than where there is an extra charge, suggesting that there may be a connection between good physical health and the feeling of relief at having health care readily available.

The disadvantage is that there is some financial risk. CCRC fees vary substantially depending on geographic location, size of unit, number of occupants, and the range of services. In 1988, the

---

*Fewer than 1% to 2% of the elderly live in CCRCs. Most of them are located in Pennsylvania, California, and Florida, with the Philadelphia-Delaware Valley area the "CCRC Capital of the World" (Somers & Spears, 1992, p. 12).

average entrance fee for a two-bedroom unit was $68,250.00; the average monthly fee was $930.00. A second occupant may cost an additional 10% to 100% (AAHA, Ernst & Young, 1989). Many people must sell their homes to raise entrance fees. Poor financial management can result in CCRC bankruptcy and residents finding themselves without homes, money, or health care. Thirty-one states have regulations to ensure careful financial planning of CCRCs and to protect consumers ("Communities," 1990).

LONG-TERM CARE AND THE CHALLENGE OF REALIZING PERSONAL VALUES

We have established that older people have individual values and aspirations and that the presence or absence of opportunities to fulfill these aspirations affects the quality of their lives. Advanced age increases the likelihood of long-term care interventions. Since most of these services are designed for groups, they tend to focus on cost-effectiveness and on serving "the greater good." Unfortunately, this means that long-term care services may actually conflict with the personal values of individuals.

The use of restraints is a clear example. Nursing homes are, above all, entrusted with protecting residents from harm. Frail nursing home residents who are prone to falls, and demented residents who wander or strike out, are often chemically or physically restrained. In a time of diminishing resources, long-term care workers are often underpaid and undertrained. Facilities may also be understaffed, which affects their ability to provide the kind of attention that enhances the human dignity of their elderly residents. Limited resources impact on quality and quantity of care, but paradoxically our institutions tend to value expensive treatments and procedures over less expensive health promotion and disease prevention programs.

Conflicts abound on all fronts. Family care is often terminated because caregivers reach a point at which they decide that they can no longer risk their own mental or physical health or jeopardize the emotional and financial well-being of their families with the burden of caregiving. So Grandma goes to the nursing home, where she must relinquish her privacy and the pleasure of a familiar environment. These are unavoidable, painful, and gut-wrenching decisions made at every level of society.

Assessing Values

An atmosphere that is completely value-friendly would be difficult to find. Even under the best of circumstances, one cannot live in accordance with every personal value all of the time. Compromises must be made. Nevertheless, if we are interested in improving the quality of life for aging Americans, attention must be given to the role of values and aspirations in their lives, in the uncovering of them, and in the development of opportunities to fulfill them.

In December 1980, the *Rand Corporation* and the University of California at Los Angeles invited experts on value preference measurement and experts on long-term care to a joint conference. The hope was that the sharing of information between these experts and the publication of their conference papers would help insert human values into long-term care decision making and thus create a more responsive system of care for the elderly (Kane & Kane, 1982). We have yet to achieve these goals.

Understanding a person's value orientation and using that knowledge to assist in long-term care decisions could dramatically affect the quality of people's lives. Liscomb (1982) points out that a hospital discharge planner might select a long-term care facility partially on the basis of which of the ADLs is most valued by the individual and what setting is most likely to promote improvement in that particular ADL.

Consumer guides could be written for retirees and for professionals to help with long-term care decision making. Such guides could include a value measurement (1) to help older adults identify their values and aspirations, and (2) to identify the settings and services that would be congruent with those values and aspirations. Hubert told me about one couple (newcomers to Franklin Village) who would have benefitted from such a guide. The couple, used to an active social life, tried to organize intimate cocktail parties and community dances. Unfortunately, such events were of no interest to most residents of Franklin Village. Eventually, the couple became unhappy with the community and transferred to a more compatible retirement community down the road.

Another potential use of value measurement could be in *program evaluation*, which would discriminate between that which works and that which doesn't work in long-term care settings and programs. Keeler and Kane (1982) suggest that this could lead to payment incentives for nursing homes that do better than average in "value achievements" (p. 96) relative to the resident's previous condition.

The development of measurements is indeed a difficult task. Administering them can be equally fraught with problems. For example, people who have been institutionalized for long periods may "forget" that there are alternatives to their everyday experience. Also, they may be reluctant to say anything about the nursing home or about their adult children that could be perceived as ungrateful or might risk arousing their caregiver's ire. Furthermore, cognitive impairments may make the results less than reliable. For some populations, behavioral measurements might have to be developed in addition to measurements that rely on verbal responses to examiner's questions.

Findings from a recent study (Cohn & Sugar, 1991) demonstrate that more than "conventional wisdom" is required to inform us about what older people value and what ultimately determines the quality of their lives. The researchers interviewed nursing home residents, their family members, staff members (physicians, nurses, social workers, activities personnel, administrators, clergy, and volunteers), and nurses' aides from several nursing homes.

The study focused on each group's definition and perception

of what constitutes quality of life inside the institution. Each group tended to rate as most important the areas over which they had some responsibility. For example, aides felt that two showers per week, proper meals, activities (to occupy residents' minds), and other forms of care ensured quality of life. Staff, aides, and family members rated health as most important. However, residents' perceptions of quality of life focused primarily on their morale and attitudes. All groups rated relatives as important, but staff rated themselves as equally important.

The researchers noted that the residents and staff tended to differ more than the residents and any other group. Because staff are likely to carry the most power in the organization, staff policies and efforts may not always be in concert with what residents consider important.

OLD AGE IN HARMONY WITH VALUES

The following section is a potpourri of ideas—my own and those of others. Several of them require setting aside old notions about what the elderly can do or how they *should* behave. They are examples of the kind of creative responses that provide older adults with opportunities to fulfill aspirations and thus enjoy a sense of well-being in the later years.

Technology

Consumer technology (e.g., VCRs and answering machines) have been slow to catch on with older Americans. This is because many of these technologies are designed to minimize social contact and save time, neither of which older people desire. They prefer contact with a human being to contact with an automatic bank teller machine. Chores provide a sense of accomplishment and independence. Older people do not want to eliminate them, only lighten or simplify them (Markle Foundation, 1989).

Computer technology, some of which is already available, has the potential for creating more meaningful and more fulfilled lives for the aged (especially for future generations of elderly who will have grown up with computers). Computers can play a major role in prolonging independence. For example, an electronic range that announces "The front burner is on," "The oven temperature is 400 degrees," or "The front door is ajar" would most likely be welcomed by visually or memory impaired elderly. A person engrossed in watching television could receive a visual message on the screen informing him or her that the cake is finished baking (Fernie, 1991). Computer dialing programs could be used to check on elderly who live alone. We might have systems connected with local health centers to monitor vital signs and conduct routine diagnostic tests. (It is already possible to use a computer modem to "hook up" an individual for monthly checkups—e.g., for a heart pacemaker.) Robotics could simplify many tasks, including cooking and cleaning, and then, as the person becomes more frail, complete the tasks for the older person (see Figure 10.1).

Driverless vehicles could be programmed to transport elderly to medical appointments, shopping areas, or social gatherings. As the person becomes more frail, voice-activated computers could help with the shopping, bill-paying, and corresponding with family and friends.

For those elderly who want to pursue personal growth and pleasure, there will be games linked by telecommunication channels and books read on microchips.*

Sunset Love

In Beijing, they call it "Sunset Love." In Taiwan, it is called a "Second Spring." Both of these governments have encouraged

---

*See Fernie (1991) for a fascinating description of the technology that is already available as well as that which will be created in the future by *engineering gerontology.*

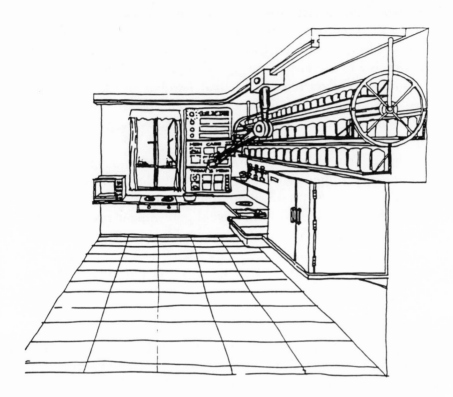

Figure 10-1. A conceptualization of a scheme to use a robotic manipulator to assist with kitchen tasks. Note the rotating storage system, the counters with unrestricted space underneath to increase wheelchair accessibility, and the electronic household systems monitoring panel, message center, and menu storage. (From "Assistive Devices, Robotics, and Quality of Life" by G. Fernie, 1991, in *The Concept and Measurement of Quality of Life in the Frail Elderly*, edited by J. Birren, J. Lubben, J. Rowe, and D. Deutchman, p. 151. Copyright © 1991 by Academic Press. Reprinted by permission.)

elderly widows and widowers to find new loves. Social workers comb the parks and community centers to find elderly who are bold enough to attend get-togethers intended to make romantic matches.

This effort, more than anything else, illustrates the changing roles of the elderly in Chinese society. At one time, age was revered. The elderly lived in multigenerational households in which their word was law and where they were assured of care. That tradition is changing as increasing numbers of young couples choose to live apart from elderly relatives. Many elderly are finding themselves rejected by their families and facing loneliness and a sense of despair. These situations present an economic strain on the government, which must assume responsibility for these older citizens.

The notion of Sunset Love and Second Spring emerged because governments became aware that elderly people (who would not be likely to survive on their own) might do very well caring for each other and thus avoid government institutionalization. For those elderly who have found new partners, the quality of life is vastly improved as they once again experience the family life-style that they value. One 73-year-old man from Taipei reported that "An old companion is worth more than a million dollars" (Huang, 1992, p. A2).

In the United States, we assume that the "young old" or "vigorous" can seek companions on their own by going to church dances or participating in senior center activities. However, this leaves out the not-so-young, not-so-healthy, and the shy. Even inside nursing homes, we might reconsider efforts to segregate male and female residents and instead *encourage* couples (heterosexual and homosexual) to share the intimacies and mutual caring that so many of the elderly value.

This includes providing for sexual and sensual expression. Unfortunately, we still harbor Victorian notions and disapproving attitudes about elderly sexuality. These attitudes inhibit life-affirming touch, affection, comfort—and passion. Many elderly in long-term care would like the pleasure of holding or of being held—if only they had a partner, a private room, and an environment that did not make them feel "depraved."

The Psychological Parent

The elderly frequently express a desire to nurture younger family members, but distance or other circumstances often make that nearly impossible. However, older adults can and do become *psychological parents* (Goldstein, Freud, & Solnit, 1979, p. 98) to younger unrelated people. For example, elderly volunteers tutor adolescents, cuddle hospitalized premature infants, and serve as foster grandparents to deprived youngsters.

A few long-term care settings have experimented with mixing the old and the young. Franklin Village, for instance, has a small day care program for the children of the staff. The children are housed in the main Center where residents can drop by and visit whenever they wish. Although it is delightful to see 80-year-olds and 2-year-olds interacting, the 80-year-olds are hardly more than casual passers-by in the children's lives. Given the opportunity, I am certain that there are residents who would be eager to become child care workers and thereby develop relationships with the children. Some child care centers (many associated with colleges and universities) are already training and hiring older adults to care for the children of the students and staff.

Valentine (1992) points out that one can have the experience of being a psychological parent or grandparent by informal mechanisms. One only has to take a folding chair out on the front step or front yard and begin to interact with nearby children or younger adults. Greetings can eventually turn to conversations that can eventually become meaningful relationships.

Archives of Human Experience

Ellis Island is a 27-acre island in Upper New York Bay that is part of the Statue of Liberty National Monument. From 1892 to 1943, it was the leading U.S. immigration center.* In 1973, the park rangers (thinking that it might be interesting to preserve the stories of the immigrants who had passed through the island) began to record informal interviews. Eventually (in 1986), the park contracted to have the interviews conducted and recorded formally and systematically. In 1989, Paul Sigrist, a social historian, was hired full-time to begin the Oral History Program at Ellis Island.

Since 1973, approximately 900 interviews have been conducted, and currently about 100 interviews per year are recorded. Those targeted for interviews are people who came through Ellis Island as immigrants, who worked on the island, or who were stationed in the military there. The primary target population, however, consists of people who immigrated prior to 1917 as adolescents (12 and older). Most of the interviewees are between 85 and 105.

There is a full recording studio on the island, although interviews are also conducted in people's homes. A nationwide network of ex-immigrants has been created through the project. Many interviewees have travelled to the island from across the country and have later gone on to do interviews for TV, newspapers, and books.

The interviews, which range in length from 30 minutes to 2 hours, are structured to include questions about life in the Old Country, the decision to immigrate (who came, and why), the actual Ellis Island experience, and the experience of adjusting to life in America.

These recordings are the repositories of experience, judgment, and wisdom. They are the fruit of decades of experience. Most of us are too immersed in the drama of everyday life to stop and reflect on our experience with objectivity and insight. These elderly orators, however, do so with fewer inhibitions than those of us with youthful pride and *ego defenses*.

---

*Approximately 17 million men, women, and children passed through its gates. In the early years, they were primarily from the United Kingdom, Germany, Scandinavia, and Switzerland. Beginning in the 1900s, there was a shift to more Southern and Eastern Europeans (Italians, Jews, Poles, Slovaks, Hungarians, Slovenians, Croatians, and Greeks) (Encyclopedia Britannica, 1992).

What purpose can these recorded histories serve? Paul Sigrist says that researchers have used the recordings to write books, plays, screenplays, and dissertations about the immigrant experience and the ethnic experience. However, oral histories can do much more. They are legacies of wisdom that reveal the ways in which people solve their problems, survive adversity, and maintain family life. They offer younger people an opportunity to discover how others have dealt with the existential questions of meaning.

Recording life experiences provides the interviewee with an opportunity to make a continuing contribution to society long after his or her death. The process of making the recording (choosing what is most important to share and giving voice to it) validates the uniqueness and worth of each life. It gives the older person a chance to integrate his or her life experience and to come to terms with both its joys and disappointments.

Why limit this experience to a few? Certainly, every life has something to teach and share. Recording one's story could become a task associated with age, like retirement or grandparenting. It could be something to look forward to, to think about from time to time, a legacy to leave behind for society.

Archives of Human Experience Centers could be set up to make these recordings in senior centers and nursing homes. Archivists could do outreach for the home-bound. We already have the technology to store vast amounts of information in small amounts of space. Just think of the advantages of being able to access the archives through a computer network. Listening to or reading the life histories of other elderly people could stimulate the memories of the old. It could provide a rich learning experience and entertainment value for young and old alike.

Contributions to the Common Good

The residents of Franklin Village frequently express altruistic aspirations. Their kindnesses to each other and to those outside the community demonstrate how much they value helping. In addition to the informal help that they and other elderly extend (e.g., shopping for a sick neighbor or helping a youngster gather autumn leaves for a school project), there are numerous formal opportunities to be helpful within the context of volunteer organizations and community groups.

One of the largest of these volunteer networks for older adults is the *Retired Senior Volunteer Program* (RSVP), in which 300,000 older people volunteer in over 700 projects (Pepper, 1981). Among the other successful national volunteer programs are the *Foster Grandparent Program* and the *Senior Companion Program*.

Unfortunately, these informal and formal helping activities are generally only appropriate for the healthy or at least "the healthy enough" older adult. What about the physically, emotionally, or mentally impaired or the bedridden who reside in the community or within institutions? They too may value helping and have no way in which to express this value.

Whatever one can do for oneself, one can do for another. By the same token, if one can be assisted in helping oneself, one can be assisted in helping another. These are simplistic statements, but they are profound in their implications. The point is that if the act of being helpful is valued, and if it contributes to the well-being of both the helper and the one receiving the help, then "value-friendly" environments should encourage and support it. It is easier for nursing home staff to water the plants in residents' rooms. A resident volunteer might spill the water, requiring a mop-up. It is more efficient to have an aide push a wheelchair than for a fragile friend to do so. It takes time and money to train elderly people to be peer counselors or literacy teachers or to be proficient in CPR.

However, it costs little to allow the elderly (frail or hardy) to do for others what they can do for themselves or to provide assistance (transportation, resources, training, etc.) so that they can continue contributing to the common good for as long as they wish.

CONCLUSION

Gone are the days when research was limited to understanding the biological processes in aging with the goal of life extension. We have been quite successful in increasing life expectancy. Now the major focus is on improving the quality of those extended lives—physically, mentally, emotionally, and spiritually.

A large proportion of elderly need long-term care services. In the next century, an unprecedented number of older Americans will join their ranks. As a result, long-term care is a concern to most Americans, and thus it has emerged as a major political issue. Resources clearly need to be developed to make long-term care services and settings accessible to everyone. Models of care will have to be developed that are flexible enough to insure that every elderly person cannot merely live, but live well—in a way that is in harmony with his or her own unique set of aspirations and values.

An old age that is in harmony with values is not totally the responsibility of policy makers, administrators of nursing homes, or other professionals and paraprofessionals. Nor does the responsibility rest totally on the shoulders of people like me, who teach, write, and conduct research. The elderly—like adults of any age—are equally responsible for the quality of their own lives. However, in order for the aged to assume that responsibility, the resources must be available to help them discover what is right for them and to fulfill those aims. Those who care about quality-of-life issues need to become sensitive to the significance of values and aspirations—and include that sensitivity and knowledge in long-term care models for the future.

GLOSSARY

acculturation—the modification or adaptation process of a group, such as a minority or immigrant group, which incorporates aspects of the dominant culture into its own existing culture.

activities of daily living (ADLs)—the performance of personal care tasks that are required for independent functioning in the community. These tasks include eating, toileting, dressing, bathing, and locomotion. The level of ability to perform these tasks is commonly used as a measure of an older person's ability to live independently. (See also *instrumental activities of daily living*.)

activity theory—the belief that, in order to age successfully, older adults should maintain as high a level of activity as possible.

adaptation—the total process of change in response to environmental conditions.

adult day care—supervised care of the physically and/or mentally impaired client during the day while his or her caregivers are at work. These medical, psychiatric, social, and/or rehabilitation services are provided in various settings: hospitals, nursing homes, social service or community agencies, churches, or free-standing enterprises.

aesthetes—people who possess a special appreciation of what is beautiful and endeavor to carry ideas of beauty into everyday life.

ageism—discrimination against people based on chronological age.

altruism—unselfish concern for the welfare of others.

Alzheimer's syndrome—the most common form of chronic brain syndrome, involving gradual, progressive brain failure over a period of 7 to 10 years. Symptoms include abnormalities in short-and long-term memory and changes in judgment, intellectual ability, activities of daily living, or personality.

analysand—a person who is being psychoanalyzed.

aspiration—a strong desire or ambition to achieve personal goal(s) in the near future, distant future, or indeterminate future. Aspirations are seen as being rooted in past, present, and future time orientations.

assimilation—the process by which a group, such as a minority group, gradually adopts the characteristics of the dominant culture.

attitudinal forces—shared beliefs and values that are culturally determined or shaped and that influence the treatment of systems, individuals, or groups.

autonomy—the maintenance of a range of life choices and the ability to govern one's own life to the maximum extent possible, given that one may rely on external resources to meet survival needs.

behavior measures—procedures that report the frequency and occurrence of a specific behavior or behaviors (e.g., how many times per week an individual participates in a recreational activity).

board and care—a type of long-term care that provides a room, meals, help with personal care activities (ADLs/IADLs), and 24-hour protection in a nonmedical smaller setting. These homes are often family owned and operated.

buffering effect—provision of a moderating force to counter a negative or potentially harmful event or circumstance.

case study—a compilation of information that includes all available data on an individual, such as written reports, ratings and diagnoses, test results, and interviews.

cohort effect—the observation that people who are born at approximately the same time share similar life experiences that may contribute to phenomena unlike those that may appear in different cohort groups.

compression of cognitive dysfunction—maintenance of intellectual functioning to the very last stage of life.

compression of morbidity—when the onset of chronic illness or diseases is postponed so that morbidity (the period of time one suffers from chronic, debilitating disease) is shortened.

consent forms—written documents to be signed by research participants that inform all potential participants about all aspects of the research that might reasonably influence their decision to participate.

content analysis—a method of transforming the contents of documents (e.g., transcribed narrative from interviews) from a qualitative, unsystematic form to a quantitative, systematic form.

continuing care retirement community (CCRC)—a form of long-term care for older persons. Residents pay an entrance fee and a monthly service fee and are provided with an apartment, meals, and a range of health-care and social services within the planned community.

control group—the subjects in an experiment who are not exposed to the experimental stimulus.

convenience samples—samples composed of subjects that are readily available and accessible to the researcher.

countertransference—a phenomenon in which a therapist or other helping professional experiences an intense emotional reaction toward a client.

CPR (cardiopulmonary resuscitation)—a procedure designed to restore normal breathing after cardiac arrest; it includes the clearance of air passages to the lungs, and heart massage by the exertion of pressure on the chest.

cross-sectional study—research based on data collected at one point in time.

crystallized intelligence—skills and information that are acquired through education, socialization, and cultural knowledge. Refers to pragmatic aspects of intelligence (i.e., the strategies or applications of knowledge).

data collection—the systemic process of gathering and recording information specific to the proposed study or research.

dementia—a condition in which there is progressive loss in intellectual capacities; it includes short- and long-term memory impairment, impaired judgment, and, in some cases, personality change.

developmental imperative—the idea that the demands of human growth and development play a major role in shaping an individual's value orientation.

direct physiological effect—that which is causally linked to changes in the functions and vital processes of a living organism.

disengagement theory—the belief that, in order for the elderly to age successfully, they and society should gradually withdraw from each other.

dual-process framework of intelligence—a theory that postulates the dual nature of intellectual functioning (fluid intelligence and crystallized intelligence).

dynamics—inner psychic forces that motivate or govern human behavior and interaction.

ego defense—the utilization of psychic energy arising from the unconscious (id) in order to protect the self (ego) from anxiety/discomfort. (This results in the creation of defense mechanisms.)

ego ideal—a set of positive standards, ideals, and ambitions that represent the way a person would like to be.

engineering gerontology—the study of gerontology from the perspective of the engineering sciences. The field would encompass the effect of technology on the aging process and the application of technology to minimize handicaps resulting from age-related impairments.

epidemiology—the sum of the factors controlling the presence of a disease or a disorder.

equilibrium—a delicate and dynamic balance found within a living system (e.g., a family).

ethnography—the science of describing a group or a culture that focuses on the predictable patterns of thought and behavior of the members of the group.

etiology—the cause of a disease or disorder.

experimental group—those subjects who are exposed to the experimental stimulus.

field experiments—experiments conducted in naturally occurring settings as people go about their everyday affairs.

field notes—detailed, descriptive accounts of observations made in a given setting.

filial piety—respect for the aged. Usually refers to a child's respect for his or her elderly parents.

fluid intelligence—the ability to impose organization on information and to generate new hypotheses. Refers to the mechanics of intelligence, such as memory operations and information processing.

focus group—a group of research subjects who meet with a researcher for the purpose of sharing their individual and collective thought on the phenomena under study.

Foster Grandparent Program—a volunteer program that gives older men and women an opportunity to transfer previous caregiving experience to surrogate grandparenting. The program matches a "grandparent" with a child who could benefit from additional adult interaction. (See Resource Directory under *Older American Volunteer Programs*.)

gatekeepers—individuals who serve to monitor and/or to restrict entry into a community or group by outsiders. Gatekeepers may be informally acknowledged or appointed or formally appointed (e.g., an institutional review board).

geriatric case management—a professional role that provides comprehensive service coordination and advocacy for older persons. This includes assessment; contracting, coordinating and monitoring appropriate services; and assistance in dealing with feelings or fears about accepting help.

gerontological research—research aimed at furthering the understanding of the aging process and/or the concerns and problems of the aged.

gerontology—the scientific study of the process of aging and the problems of aged people.

Hemlock Society—an organization that supports suicide under certain circumstances and the decriminalization of assistance to a person who makes that decision.

high morale—a positive mental condition in which one experiences a feeling of well-being and a sense of purpose and optimism about the future.

homogeneity—the status of sharing the same defining qualities or characteristics.

human science approach (also *qualitative research*)—an approach whose purpose is to understand human meaning and experience with an emphasis on direct human contact, the subjective experience of the subjects under study, and the use of linguistic (written or verbal) and observational data. (See also *qualitative approach*.)

hypothesis—a testable statement of presumed relationship between two or more concepts.

identity crisis—a period of tension in which an individual struggles to establish a secure sense of self and personality and to understand expected functions and behaviors in the social context.

identity—a consolidated sense of who one is; individuality and a sense of self.

in-depth interview—a face-to-face conversation in which the purpose is to understand the interviewee's inner feelings and experiences; questions are designed to obtain the subjective view of the interviewee.

independence—able to function without relying on something or someone else for one's existence.

informants—subjects who are more articulate and culturally aware or more insightful than others, thus playing a pivotal role in research by providing an insider's perspective on the community.

inner experience—the mental representation of life experience; the process of reviewing, interpreting, and giving meaning to life events and experiences; and the process of planning for new life events.

institutional ageism—the process by which the policy of an institution or a social structure discriminates against people because of their chronological age.

institutional review board (IRB)—also called a *human subject committee*. IRBs overview and oversee research projects and act to protect human subjects. They have the authority to approve, disapprove, or modify research activities.

instrumental activities of daily living (IADLs)—those daily activities that enhance independent functioning in the community. These tasks include cooking, cleaning, doing laundry, transporting oneself, reading, writing, and managing money.

instrumental values—specific ways of acting or being; modes of conduct.

instruments—tools such as interviews or questionnaires used by researchers to measure specific phenomena.

learning theory—the notion that behavior is motivated by rewards and punishments.

level of activity—amount of involvement with family and friends, participation in organizations or groups, and pursuit of hobbies, interests, and activities.

life expectancy—the average number of years from birth to death as based on statistical analyses of the length of life for people born in a particular period.

life review—a process of increased introspection, reflection, and recounting of the past often undertaken by older people. This process of reminiscence is understood as a means to recast painful past events or to re-experience positive past events in the face of loss of youth and proximity to death.

living wills—legal documents that direct what procedures (if any) might be used to prolong life. The directive that no extraordinary measures be taken is often stated.

long-term care—the array of services (health, personal care, and social services) that are needed on a continuing basis to enable people with chronic disabilities to maintain their physical, social, and psychological functioning. These services are provided both formally and informally in institutions, in community settings, and in family or social networks.

longitudinal study—research based on data gathered over an extended period of time.

maintainers—those retirement-community members whose primary interest is to maintain the pleasure they derive in the present.

masculine protest—a response in which an individual compensates for feelings of inferiority by being physically or sexually aggressive.

Meals on Wheels—a meal delivery program to homebound individuals that provides one or two meals per day. Volunteers, often older people themselves, prepare and deliver the meals, and serve the additional function of providing social contact.

Medicaid—social program that provides health insurance to the very poor, regardless of age. It is funded jointly by state and federal governments and is administered through local welfare departments.

metaparadigm—an abstract framework or philosophy that may guide more discrete conceptual models.

mirror gazing—a process by which elderly people, upon catching their reflections in the mirror, are propelled into a course of preoccupation with past deeds.

modernization theory—an argument that structural forces, primarily industrialization and urbanization, are responsible for a negative change in the way older persons are regarded in society.

morbidity—the period of time one suffers from chronic, debilitating disease.

multilevel facility—housing projects, such as *continuing care retirement communities*, that offer a range of services, from independent to congregate living arrangements, from intermediate to skilled care facilities.

neurotic behavior—according to Adler (Ansbacher & Ansbacher, 1956), all behavior that fuctions to safeguard an individual's self-esteem and is directed toward achieving the goal of superiority.

normal aging—biological and psychological changes that are irreversible, progress over time, and have an effect on the individual's functioning.

nursing home—a type of long-term care that is highly institutionalized and where medical and social services are provided on-site.

objective measure—a way of determining changes or movement that is based in fact or physical reality and which is independent of the observer or the subjective experience.

old-old—among the very old, those who have suffered major physical or mental decrements.

operationalize—to provide definitions for concepts that indicate the precise procedures or operations to be followed in measuring the concept.

organ dialect—a response in which an individual compensates for feelings of inferiority with real or feigned disability.

paradigm—a model or conceptual framework.

participant-observation—a method in which the researcher is a part of, and participates in, the activities of the people, group, or situation that is being studied.

personal ageism—negative beliefs and attitudes about age that are held by individuals and that result in discrimination against others.

personal growth—a value that stimulates the desire for spiritual and intellectual self-improvement.

physiological imperative—the idea that the basic needs for food, water, and protection from the elements play a prerequisite role in the shaping of value orientations.

post-test results—findings from data gathered and measured following an experiment or intervention. These findings demonstrate the effects of the experiment.

pretest results—findings from a preliminary series of data gathering and measurement. These findings establish baseline scores for the phenomena under investigation.

program evaluation—a research approach designed to provide feedback about current program functioning; it can be used to modify and improve program operations. This approach also can assess the effectiveness of particular programs in meeting established goals and objectives.

psychological parents—people who have the experiences of parenting—nurturing, advising, teaching—younger people. For older people, this experience can be gained either formally through volunteer programs (e.g., *Foster Grandparent Program*) or informally through contact with friends, neighbors, or extended family.

qualitative approach (qualitative research methodology)—research that produces findings not arrived at by means of statistical or quantified procedures. The purpose of the research is to understand human meaning and experience and the subjective experience of the subject, using linguistic (verbal or written) and observational data. (See also *human science approach.*)

quality of life—an important component of successful aging that encompasses adequate material resources and perceptions of self-worth. Crucial components of perceived quality of life include life satisfaction, self-esteem, general health, functional status, and socioeconomic status.

quantitative approach (quantitative research methodology)—research that produces findings arrived at by means of statistical, quantified procedures and that seeks facts or causal relationships.

Rand Corporation—a foundation whose primary function is to conduct research.

random sample—a sample in which each element in the target population has an equal probability of being chosen for the sample.

re-creators—those who desire and attempt to recall and re-experience events from earlier in life so that they may once again enjoy the feelings that were associated with these former activities.

recreationalists—retirement-community members whose primary social role is that of participation in leisure-time activities.

reframe—to redefine a problem in a more positive way.

regression—the mechanism by which a person reverts to the functioning of a much younger, more dependent, childlike individual.

relaxers—retirement-community members whose primary social role is to enjoy simple, calm activities such as reading and taking time to notice those things they haven't had time to enjoy earlier in life.

rescue behavior—a kind of helping behavior in which the individual moves to share the pain, discomfort, or potential danger on behalf of another.

Retired Senior Volunteer Program (RSVP)—a volunteer program that places older volunteers to work in schools, courts, libraries, day-care centers, hospitals, and community service centers. (See Resource Directory under *Older American Volunteer Programs.*)

retirement hotel—a living facility for older persons who do not need or desire skilled nursing care. It is often a converted hotel or apartment building; there may be a common dining room and kitchen and limited services (housekeeping, social programs). Most are operated by private nonprofit *and* profitmaking corporations.

right to die—the belief that individuals should be allowed to choose to end life or refuse life-prolonging treatments if they are suffering.

self-fulfilling prophecy—the tendency for individuals or groups to become what others expect them to be or what they expect themselves to be.

Senior Companion Program—a volunteer program in which older volunteers help other older persons remain in their own homes or provide extra support when they have special health and social needs. (See Resource Directory under *Older American Volunteer Programs.*)

snowball sampling—a type of nonprobability sampling in which a few cases of the type we wish to study lead to more cases, who in turn lead to still more cases, until a sufficient sample is built up.

social exchange theory—the theory that individuals help one another because they believe that the help given is proportional to the help that will be received or is expected to be received.

social support system—a structure that leads a person to believe that he or she is cared for and loved, is esteemed and valued, and belongs to a network of communication, support, and mutual obligation.

social values—the basic values, or beliefs, held as desirable by a society, which are reflected in social institutions and attitudes.

sociocultural imperative—the idea that social values play a major role in shaping an individual's value orientation.

spend down—to deplete one's assets and life savings.

spiritual well-being—the affirmation of life in a relationship with a god, self, community, or environment that nurtures and celebrates wholeness. (Adapted from the National Interfaith Coalition on Aging [1975].)

spirituality—the experience of searching for deep meaning and purpose in life, a meaning connected to the supernatural or that which transcends bodily existence.

stage theory—personal growth that occurs throughout the life span in specific discrete periods, or stages. These stages each provide a central task to achieve or conflict to resolve.

statistical analysis—procedures for assembling, classifying, and tabulating numerical data so that some meaning, measurement, or information is derived.

structural forces—elements pertaining to the organization of society, such as industrialization or urbanization, that influence the individuals or groups who make up the society.

subjective measures—ways of determining change or movement that are based upon the self-reported feelings, perceptions, or experiences of the individual(s) under study.

suppression—a mechanism by which a person "pushes" unpleasant emotions from awareness.

terminal values—specific ways of existing pertaining to end-states or outcomes.

tests of significance—statistical methods designed to measure the degree to which an obtained value will not occur by chance and can therefore be attributed to another variable, specifically variables being researched.

transference—a common phenomenon in which one transfers feelings and attitudes toward a person from the past to a present relationship.

value conflict (or *value dilemma*)—the experience of a period of transition in the prioritization of values (value orientation or value hierarchy) that is characterized by feelings of uncertainty, anxiety, or guilt.

value hierarchy (or *value orientation*)—an individual's arrangement of personal values such that specific values are prioritized or rank-ordered. These value systems may shift according to priority over time.

value orientation (see *value hierarchy*)

values—personal beliefs that motivate action.

young-old—among the very old, those who remain healthy, vigorous, and competent.

REFERENCES

Adler, A. (1930). Individual psychology. In C. Murchinson (Ed.), *Psychologies of 1930* (pp. 395–408). Worcester, MA: Clark University Press.

Adler, A. (1956). *The individual psychology of Alfred Adler* (H. L. Ansbacher & R. R. Ansbacher, Eds.). New York: Basic Books.

Ahmed, S. M., Kraft, I. A., & Porter, D. M. (1987). Attitudes of different professional groups toward geriatric patients. *Gerontology and Geriatric Education*, 6, 77–86.

American Association of Homes for the Aging & Ernst & Young (1989). *Continuing care retirement communities: An industry in action: Analysis and developing trends in 1989*. Washington, DC: The Association.

American Association of Retired Persons. (1990). *Understanding senior housing*. Washington, DC: Author.

American Association of Retired Persons. (1991). *Before you buy: A guide to long-term care insurance*. Washington, DC: Author.

Ansbacher, H. L., & Ansbacher, R. R. (Eds.). (1956). See Adler (1956).

Babigian, H. M., & Lehman, A. F. (1987). Functional psychosis in later life: Epidemiological patterns from the Monroe County psychiatric register. In N. E. Miller & G. D. Cohen (Eds.), *Schizophrenia and aging* (pp. 9–21). New York: Guilford.

Back, K. W., & Bogdonoff, M. D. (1967). Buffer conditions in experimental stress. *Behavior Science*, 12, 384–390.

Baltes, P. B., Smith, J., Staudinger, U. M., & Sowarka, D. (1990). Wisdom: One facet of successful aging. In M. Perlmutter (Ed.), *Late life potential* (pp. 63–81). New York: Springer Publishing Company.

Beck, M. (1990, Winter-Spring). The geezer boom; in old age, as in youth, the baby boom will shake society by the sheer strength of its numbers. *Newsweek* (Special Edition: The 21st Century Family), pp. 62–65.

Birren, J. E. (1964). *Handbook of the psychology of aging*. Englewood Cliffs, NJ: Prentice Hall.

Bloom, J. (1982). Social support systems and cancer: A conceptual view. In J.

Cohen, J. Cullen, & R. Martin (Eds.), *Psychosocial aspects of cancer* (pp. 129–149). New York: Raven Press.

Brink, T. L. (1979). *Geriatric psychotherapy.* New York: Human Sciences Press.

Brummel-Smith, K. (1986). Interviewing the older adult. In A. J. Enlow & S. N. Swisher (Eds.), *Interviewing and patient care* (pp. 148–162). New York: Oxford University Press.

Buhler, C. (1935). The curve of life as studied in biographies. *Journal of Applied Psychology, 19,* 405–409.

Butler, R. N. (1963). The life review: An interpretation of reminiscence in the aged. *Psychiatry, 26,* 65–76.

Butler, R. N. (1969). Age-ism: Another form of bigotry. *The Gerontologist, 9,* 243–246.

Butler, R. N. (1975). *Why survive?* New York: Harper & Row.

Butler, R. N. (1980). The life review: An unrecognized bonanza. *International Journal of Aging and Human Development, 12,* 35–38.

Butler, R. N. (1989). Dispelling ageism: The cross-cutting intervention. *Annals of the American Academy of Political and Social Science, 503,* 138–147.

Butler, R. N., & Lewis, M. I. (1988). *Love and sex after 60.* New York: Harper & Row.

Butler, R. N., Lewis, M. I., & Sunderland, T. (1991). *Aging and mental health: Positive psychosocial and biomedical approaches.* New York: Macmillian.

Cassel, J. (1976). The contribution of the social environment to host resistance. *American Journal of Epidemiology, 104,* 107–123.

Cattell, R. B. (1971). *Abilities: Their structure, growth and action.* Boston: Houghton Mifflin.

Chappell, N. L., & Badger, M. (1989). Social isolation and well-being. *Journal of Gerontology, 44*(5), 169–176.

Cheung, L. Y. S., Cho, E. R., Lum, D., Tang, T. Y., & Yau, H. B. (1980). The Chinese elderly and family structure: Implications for health care. *Public Health Reports, 95*(5), 491–495.

Chinen, A. B. (1991). The return of wonder in old age. *Generations, 15*(2), 45–48.

Cobb, S. (1976). Social support as a moderator of life stress. *Psychosomatic Medicine, 38,* 300–314.

Cohen, S., & Syme, L. S. (1985). Issues in the study and application of social support. In S. Cohen & L. S. Syme (Eds.), *Social support and health* (pp. 1–20). Orlando, FL: Academic Press.

Cohn, J., & Sugar, J. A. (1991). Determinants of quality of life in institutions: Perception of frail older residents, staff and family. In J. E. Birren, J. E. Lubben, J. C. Rowe, & D. E. Deutchman (Eds.), *The concept of quality of life in the frail elderly* (pp. 28–49). New York: Academic Press.

Cole, T. R. (1979). The ideology of old age and death in American history. *American Quarterly, XXXI,* 223–231.

Cole, T. R. (1983). The "enlightened" view of aging: Victorian morality in a new key. *The Hastings Center Report*, *13*(2), 34–40.

Colerick, E. J., & George, L. K. (1986). Predictors of institutionalization among caregivers of patients with Alzheimer's disease. *Journal of the American Geriatrics Society*, *34*, 493–498.

Collopy, B. J. (1990). Ethical dimensions of autonomy in long-term care. *Generations*, *14* (Suppl. 1990), 9–12.

Communities for the Elderly. (1990, February). *Consumer Reports*, pp. 123–131.

Covey, H. C. (1985). Qualitative research on older people: Some considerations. *Gerontology and Geriatrics Education*, *5*(3), 41–50.

Crawford, G. (1987). Support networks and health-related change in the elderly: Theory-based nursing strategies. *Family and Community Health*, *10*, 39–48.

Cuellar, J. (1978). El seniors citizens club: The older Mexican-American in the voluntary association. In B. G. Myerhoff & A. Simić (Eds.), *Life's career— aging: Cultural variations on growing old* (pp. 207–230). Newbury Park, CA: Sage.

Cumming, E., & Henry, W. D. (1961). *Growing old*. New York: Basic Books.

Doehrman, S. (1977). Psychological aspects of recovery from coronary heart disease: A review. *Social Science and Medicine*, *11*, 199–218.

Dorfman, R. A. (1988). *Paradigms of clinical social work*. New York: Brunner/Mazel.

Dowd, J. J. (1980). Exchange rates and old people. *Journal of Gerontology*, *35*(4), 596–602.

Dychtwald, K., & Flower, J. (1989). *Age wave*. Los Angeles: Jeremy P. Tarcher.

Eglit, H. (1989). Ageism in the workplace: An elusive quarry. *Generations: Journal of the American Society on Aging*, *XIII*(2), 31–35.

Eid, J. F., & Pearce, C. (1993). *Making love again: Regaining sexual potency through the new injection treatment*. New York: Brunner/Mazel.

Eidelberg, L. (1973). Ego-ideal. *The encyclopedia of psychoanalysis*. New York: The Free Press.

Eisenhandler, S. A. (1990). The asphalt identikit: Old age and the driver's license. *International Journal of Aging and Human Development*, *30*(1), 1–14.

Ekerdt, D. J. (1986). The busy ethic: Moral continuity between work and retirement. *The Gerontologist*, *26*(3), 239–244.

Ell, K. (1984). Social networks, social support and health status: A review. *Social Service Review*, *58*, 133–149.

Ellison, G. W. (1983). Spiritual well-being: Conceptualization and measurement. *Journal of Psychology and Theology*, *11*(4), 330–340.

Encyclopedia Britannica. (1992). Vol. 4, p. 460. Chicago: Encyclopedia Britannica, Inc.

Epstein, A. (1933). *Insecurity: A challenge to America*. New York: Smith and Hass.

Erikson, E. H. (1963). *Childhood and society* (2nd. ed.). New York: W. W. Norton & Company.

Fernie, G. (1991). Assistive devices, robotics, and quality of life in the frail elderly. In J. E. Birren, J. E. Lubben, J. C. Rowe, & D. E. Deutchman (Eds.), *The concept and measurement of quality of life in the frail elderly* (pp. 142–167). New York: Academic Press.

Fischer, D. H. (1978). *Growing old in America* (exp. ed.). New York: Oxford University Press.

Ford, C. V., & Sbordone, R. J. (1980). Attitudes of psychiatrists toward elderly patients. *American Journal of Psychiatry, 137*, 571–575.

French, J. R. P., Rodgers, W., & Cobb, S. (1974). Adjustment as person-environment fit. In D. Coehlo, A. Hamburg, & D. Adams (Eds.), *Coping and adaptation* (pp. 316–333). New York: Basic Books.

Freud, S. (1922). *Beyond the pleasure principle*. London: Hogarth Press.

Freud, S. (1924). *Collected papers* (Vol. 1). London: Hogarth Press.

Fries, J. F. (1980). Aging, natural death, and the compression of morbidity. *New England Journal of Medicine, 303*(3), 130–135.

Goldmeier, J. (1986). Pets or people: Another research note. *The Gerontologist, 26*, 203–206.

Goldstein, J., Freud, A., & Solnit, A. J. (1979). *Beyond the best interest of the child*. New York: The Free Press.

Gratton, B. (1985). Factories, attitudes, and the new deal: The history of old age. In B. B. Hess & E. W. Markson (Eds.), *New perspectives on old age* (3rd ed., pp. 28–44). New Brunswick, NJ: Transaction Books.

Grotjahn, M. (1982). The day I got old. *Psychiatric Clinics of North America, 5*, 233–237.

Gurland, B. J., & Cross, P. S. (1982). Epidemiology of psychopathology in old age. In L. Jarvick & G. Small (Eds.), *Psychiatric clinics of North America* (pp. 11–26). Philadelphia: Saunders.

Havighurst, R. J., & Albrecht, R. (1953). *Older people*. New York: David McKay.

Hinrichsen, G. A. (1990). *Mental health problems and older adults: Choices and challenges*. Santa Barbara, CA: ABC-CLIO, Inc.

Horn, J. L. (1970). Organization of data on life-span development of human abilities. In L. R. Goulet & P. B. Baltes (Eds.), *Life-span developmental psychology: Research and theory* (pp. 423–466). New York: Academic Press.

House, J. S., Landis, K. R., & Umberson, D. (1988). Social relationships and health. *Science, 241*, 540–545.

Huang, A. (1992, February 2). "Second spring" urged for Taiwan's elderly. *Los Angeles Times*, p. A2.

Humphry, D. (1991). *Final exit: The practicalities of self-deliverance and assisted suicide for the dying*. Eugene, OR: The Hemlock Society.

Jerome, D. (1981). The significance of friendship in later life. *Aging and Society, 1*, 175–197.

Kahana, E. A. (1975). Consequence model of person-environment interaction. In T. O. Byerts, M. P. Lawton, & J. Neucomber (Eds.), *Theory development in environments and aging* (pp. 97–120), Washington, DC: Gerontological Society.

Kahana, E., & Midlarsky, E. (1983). Perspectives on helping in late life: Conceptual and empirical directions. *Academic Psychology Bulletin, 5*, 351–361.

Kalish, R. A. (1979). The new ageism and the failure models: A polemic. *The Gerontologist, 19*, 398–402.

Kane, R. A., & Kane, R. L. (Eds.). (1982). *Values and long-term care.* Toronto: Lexington Books.

Kane, R. A., & Kane, R. L. (1987). *Long-term care: Principles, progress and policies.* New York: Springer.

Kastenbaum, R. (1991). The creative impulse: Why it won't just quit. *Generations, 15*(2), 7–12.

Kastenbaum. R. J. (1973). Loving, dying and other gerontological addenda. In C. Eisdorfer, L. Eisdorfer, & M. Powell (Eds.), *The psychology of adult development and aging* (pp. 699–708). Washington, DC: American Psychological Association.

Katz, R. S. (1990). Using our emotional reactions to older clients: A working theory. In B. Genevay & R. S. Katz (Eds.), *Countertransference and older clients* (pp. 17–26). New York: Sage Publications.

Katz, S., Downs, T. D., Cash, H., & Grotz, R. C. (1970). Progress and development of the index of ADL. *The Gerontologist, 10*, 20–30.

Katz, S., Ford, A. B., Moskowitz, R. W., Jackson, B. A., & Jaffe, M. W. (1963). Studies of illness in the aged: The index of ADL. A standardized measure of biological function. *Journal of the American Medical Association, 185*, 914–919.

Kaufman, S. R. (1986). *The ageless self.* New York: Meridian.

Keeler, E., & Kane, R. (1982). What is special about long-term care? In R. L. Kane & R. A. Kane (Eds.), *Values and long-term care (pp. 85–99).* Toronto: Lexington Books.

Keith, J. (1980). Participant observation. In C. L. Fry & J. Keith (Eds.), *New methods for old age research: Anthropological alternatives* (pp. 8–26). Chicago: Center for Urban Policy.

Kenworthy, L. S. (1987). *Think on these things: An anthology of inspirational quotations.* Philadelphia: Friendly Press.

Kenworthy, L. S. (1988). *Going to meeting* (pamphlet). Philadelphia: Religious Society of Friends.

Kluckhohn, C. (1951). Values and value orientations in the theory of action. In

T. Parsons & E. A. Shils (Eds.), *Toward a general theory of action* (pp. 388–433), Cambridge, MA: Harvard University Press.

Kohlberg, L. (1976). Moral stages and moralization: The cognitive developmental approach. In T. Lickona (Ed.), *Moral development and behavior: Theory, research, and social issues* (pp. 31–53). New York: Holt, Rinehart and Winston.

Kroll, K., & Klein, E. L. (1992). *Enabling romance*. New York: Harmony Books.

Kuhn, M. (1991, September 22). Getting beyond old. *Philadelphia Inquirer Magazine*, pp. 14–29.

Langer, E. J. (1989). *Mindfulness*. New York: Addison-Wesley.

Langer, E., & Rodin, J. (1976). The effects of enhanced personal responsibility for the aged: A field experiment in an institutional setting. *Journal of Personality and Social Psychology, 34*, 191–198.

Larson, R., Mannell, R., & Zuzanek, J. (1986). Daily well-being of older adults with friends and family. *Psychology and Aging, 1*, 117–126.

Lasch, C. (1978). The culture of narcissism: American life in an age of diminishing expectations. New York: W. W. Norton.

Laurie, W. (1987). Federal expenditures, year 2000. In G. Maddox (Ed.), *The encyclopedia of aging* (p. 255). New York: Springer Publishing Company.

Lawton, M. P. (1977). Morale: What are we measuring? In C. N. Nydegger (Ed.), *Measuring morale: A guide to effective assessment* (pp. 4–6). Washington, DC: Gerontological Society.

Lawton, M. P., & Brody, E. M. (1969). Assessment of older people: Self-maintenance and instrumental activities of daily living. *The Gerontologist, 9*, 176–186.

Lawton, M. P., & Hoffman, C. (1984). Neighborhood reactions to elderly housing. *Journal of Housing for the Elderly, 2*, 41–53.

Levinson, D. (1978). *The seasons of a man's life*. New York: Knopf.

Lewin, K. (1951). *Field theory in social science*. New York: Harper.

Lewis, M. I., & Butler, R. N. (1974, November). Life review therapy: Putting memories to work in individual and group psychotherapy. *Geriatrics, 29*, 165–173.

Lewittes, H. J. (1988). Just being friendly means a lot—Women, friendship, and aging. *Women and Health, 14*, 139–159.

Lindeman, B. (1987). Let's get serious about age biases. *Fifty Plus, 27*(10), 4–5.

Linkletter, A. (1985). *Old age is not for sissies*. New York: Penguin Books.

Liscomb, J. (1982). Value preferences for health: Meaning, measurement, and use in program evaluation. In R. L. Kane & R. A. Kane (Eds.), *Values and long-term care* (pp. 27–67). Toronto: Lexington Books.

Loevinger, J. (1976). *Ego development*. San Francisco: Jossey-Bass.

Lowenthal, M. F., Thurnher, M., & Chiriboga, D. (1975). *Four stages of life*. San Francisco: Jossey-Bass.

Lubben, J. E. (1988). Assessing social networks among elderly populations. *Family and Community Health*, 8, 42–52.

Lynch, J. J. (1979). *The broken heart*. New York: Basic Books.

Markle Foundation. (1989). *Pioneers on the frontiers of life: Aging in America*. New York: The Markle Foundation. (Report of a study of older Americans' values, beliefs, behavior, and overall outlook on life. Available from The Markle Foundation, 75 Rockefeller Plaza, New York, NY 10019.)

Maslow, A. H. (1954). *Motivation & personality*. New York: Harper Brothers.

Maslow, A. H. (1968). *Toward a psychology of being* (2nd ed.). New York: Van Nostrand Reinhold.

Maslow, A. H. (1970). *Motivation & personality* (2nd ed.). New York: Harper & Row.

Moody, H. R. (1989). Gerontology with a human face. In L. E. Thomas (Ed.), *Research on adulthood and aging: The human science approach* (pp. 227–240). New York: State University of New York Press.

Moroney, R. M. (1980). *Families, social service, and social policy: The issue of shared responsibility*. Washington, DC: U.S. Department of Health and Human Services.

Morycz, R. (1985). Caregiving strain and the desire to institutionalize family members with Alzheimer's disease. *Research on Aging*, 7, 329–361.

Murray, H. A. (1938). *Explorations in personality: A clinical and experimental study of fifty men of college age*. New York: Oxford University Press.

Myerhoff, B. G. (1978). *Number our days*. New York: Simon and Schuster.

Myerhoff, B. G., & Simić, A. (Eds.). (1978). *Life's career—aging: Cultural variations on growing old*. Newbury Park, CA: Sage.

National Center for Health Statistics. (1987). Use of nursing homes by the elderly: Preliminary data from the 1985 nursing home survey. *Advance data from vital and health statistics* (No. 135). (DHHS Publication No. PHS 87–1250.) Hyattsville, MD: Public Health Service.

National Center for Health Statistics. (1986). *Health, United States, 1986*. (DHHS Publication No. PHS 87–1232.) Washington, DC: Department of Health and Human Services.

National Interfaith Coalition on Aging, Inc. (1975). *Spiritual well-being: A definition*. Washington, DC: Author.

Needleman, J. (1987). *The new religions*. New York: Crossroad Publishing Co.

Neidhardt, E. R., & Allen, J. (1993). *Family therapy with the elderly*. New York: Sage Publications.

Older Women's League. (1986). *Death and dying: Staying in control to the end of our lives*. Washington, DC: Author.

Osgood, N. J. (1983). Patterns of aging in retirement communities: Typologies of residents. *Journal of Applied Gerontology*, 2, 23–43.

Oxford English Dictionary (2nd. ed.). (1989). Aesthetes. Oxford: Clarendon Press.

Palmore, E. (1978). When can age, period and cohort be separated? *Social Forces*, 57, 282.

Palmore, E. (1981). *Social patterns in normal aging*. Durham, NC: Duke University Press.

Palmore, E. (1990). *Ageism: Negative and positive*. New York: Springer Publishing Company.

Peck, R. C. (1968). Psychological developments in the second half of life. In B. L. Neugarten (Ed.), *Middle age and aging* (pp. 88–92). Chicago: University of Chicago Press.

Pepper, C. (1981). Senior volunteerism: Alive and well in the 80s. *Generations, 4*, 6–7.

Perlmutter, M. (1988). Cognitive potential throughout life. In J. Birren & V. Bengston (Eds.), *Emergent theories of aging* (pp. 247–268). New York: Springer Publishing Company.

Polman, D. (1989, August 20). And now, a word from our sponsors: Older. *Philadelphia Inquirer*, p. 1-A.

Reichstein, K. J., & Bergofsky, L. (1983). Domiciliary care facilities for adults: An analysis of state regulations. *Research on Aging, 5*, 25–43.

Reuben, D. B., Silliman, R. A., & Traines, M. (1988). The aging driver: Medicine, policy and ethics. *Journal of the American Gerontological Society, 36*, 1135–1142.

Rodin, J., & Langer, E. (1977). Long-term effects of a control-relevant intervention among the institutionalized aged. *Journal of Personality and Social Psychology, 35*, 275–282.

Rokeach, M. (1968). *Beliefs, attitudes, and values: A theory of organization and change*. San Francisco: Jossey-Bass.

Rokeach, M. (1973). *The nature of human values*. New York: Free Press.

Russell, J., & Editors of Time-Life Books. (1969). *The world of Matisse: 1869–1954*. New York: Time-Life Books.

Ryff, C. D. (1989). In the eye of the beholder: Views of psychological well-being among middle-aged and older adults. *Psychology and Aging, 4*(2), 195–210.

Salthouse, T. A. (1984). Effects of age and skill on typing. *Journal of Experimental Psychology: General, 113*, 345–371.

Scott, W. A. (1965). *Values and organizations: A study of fraternities and sororities*. Chicago: Rand McNally.

Schaie, K. E. (Ed.). (1983). *Longitudinal studies of adult psychological development*. New York: Guilford Press.

Simić, A. (1978). Winners and losers: Aging Yugoslavs in a changing world. In B. G. Myerhoff & A. Simić (Eds.), *Life's career—aging: Cultural variations on growing old* (pp. 77–106). Newbury Park, CA: Sage.

Simić, A. (1987). Ethnicity as a career for the elderly: The Serbian-American case. *Journal of Applied Gerontology, 6*(1), 113–126.

Simonton, D. K. (1988). Age and outstanding achievement: What do we know after a century of research? *Psychological Bulletin*, *104*, 251–267.

Simonton, D. K. (1989). The swan-song phenomenon: Last-works effects for 172 classical composers. *Psychology and Aging*, *4*, 42–47.

Simonton, D. K. (1990). Creativity in the later years: Optimistic prospects for achievement. *The Gerontologist*, *30*, 626–631.

Sokolovsky, J. (1983). *Growing old in different societies*. Belmont, CA: Wadsworth.

Soldo, B., & Manton, K. (1985). Health status and service needs of the oldest old: Current patterns and future trends. *Milbank Memorial Fund Quarterly/Health and Society*, *63*, 286–319.

Somers, A. R., & Spears, N. L. (1992). *The continuing care retirement community: A significant option for long-term care?* New York: Springer Publishing Company.

Starr, B., & Weiner, M. (1981). *Sex and sexuality in the mature years*. New York: McGraw-Hill.

Staudinger, U. M., Cornelius, S. W., & Baltes, P. B. (1989, May). The aging of intelligence: Potential and limits. *Annals of the American Academy of Political and Social Science*, *503*, 43–59.

Thoits, P. A. (1982). Conceptual, methodological, and theoretical problems in studying social support as a buffer against life stress. *Journal of Health and Social Behavior*, *23*, 145–159.

Thomas, L. E. (1989). The human science approach to understanding adulthood and aging. In L. E. Thomas (Ed.), *Research on adulthood and aging: The human science approach* (pp. 1–10). New York: State University of New York Press.

Thomas, L. E., & Chambers, K. O. (1989). Successful aging among elderly men in England and India: A phenomenological comparison. In L. E. Thomas (Ed.), *Research on adulthood and aging: The human science approach* (pp. 183–204). New York: State University of New York Press.

Turner, F. J. (Ed.). (1992). *Mental health and the elderly: A social work perspective*. New York: Free Press.

U.S. Bureau of the Census. (1989). Projections of the population of the United States, by age, sex, and race: 1988 to 2080. U. S. Current Population Reports, Series P-25 (No. 1018). Washington, DC: U.S. Government Printing Office.

U.S. Bureau of the Census. (1990). Summary Tape File–1A.

U.S. Department of Labor. (1965, June). *The older American worker, age discrimination in employment* (Report of Secretary of Labor to the Congress under Section 715 of the Civil Rights Act of 1964). Washington, DC: U. S. Government Printing Office.

U.S. Senate Special Committee on Aging. (1988). *Aging America: Trends and projections*. Washington, DC: U.S. Department of Health and Human Services.

Valentine, J. (1992, February 22). [Interview on "Family Matters" radio show]. (Cassette available from WHHY-91 FM, 150 N. 6th St., Philadelphia, PA: 19106).

Viney, L. L., Benjamin, Y. N., & Preston, C. (1989). Mourning and reminiscence: Parallel psychotherapeutic processes for elderly people. *International Journal of Aging and Human Development, 28,* 239–249.

Wagner, G., & Kaplan, H. S. (1993). *The new injection treatment for impotence: Medical and psychological aspects.* New York: Brunner/Mazel.

Whitman, W. (1931). *Leaves of grass.* New York: Arentine Press.

Williams, S. (1985). Long-term care alternatives: Continuing care retirement communities. *Journal of Housing for the Elderly, 3*(1/2), 15–34.

Winklevoss, H. A. (1985). Continuing care retirement communities: Issues in financial management and actuarial prediction. *Journal of Housing for the Elderly, 3*(1/2), 57–64.

Wolinsky, M. A. (1990). A heart of wisdom: Marital counseling with older and elderly couples. New York: Brunner/Mazel.

Wong, B. P. (1979). *A Chinese American community: Ethnicity and survival strategies.* Singapore: Chopmen Enterprises.

Yalom, I. D. (1980). *Existential psychotherapy.* New York: Basic Books.

RESOURCES

Note: Additional resources may be listed in a community's telephone directory (often in a special section in the back, or in the "blue pages") under "Social Service Agencies" or under U.S., state, or local government listings.

PROFESSIONAL ORGANIZATIONS

Alliance for Aging Research, 2021 K St., NW, Suite 305, Washington, DC 20006-1003. (202) 293-2856 Professional membership organization. Network of professionals researching salient aging issues. Leading advocacy organization for promoting health and independence of older Americans. Sponsors conferences; publishes newsletters on research, grants, and opportunities.

American Association for Geriatric Psychiatry, P.O. Box 376-A, Greenbelt, MD 20768. (301) 220-0952 Professional organization of psychiatrists interested in mental health of older people. Informs members about research developments; monitors certification requirements for geriatric psychiatrists; publishes newsletter.

American Association of Homes for the Aging, 901 E St., NW, Suite 500, Washington, DC 20004-2037. (202) 783-2242 FAX: (202) 783-2255 Professional membership organization. Represents nonprofit organizations that provide health care, housing, and services to the elderly. Represents members in legislative issues; publishes newsletter.

American Bar Association, Commission on the Legal Problems of the Elderly, Second Floor, South Lobby, 1800 M St., NW, Washington, DC

20036. (202) 331-2297   FAX: (202) 331-2220   Professional organization. Analyzes and responds to the law-related needs of older persons; supports community organizations that provide low-cost legal aid to older people. Provides continuing education for attorneys; publishes quarterly journal.

American Federation for Aging Research, 1414 Avenue of the Americas, 18th Fl., New York, NY 10019. (212) 752-2327 FAX: (212) 832-2298   Private nonprofit voluntary organization supporting research aimed at age-related diseases and disabilities. Funds biomedical studies; sponsors meetings and conferences; publishes newsletter.

American Society for Geriatric Dentistry, 211 E. Chicago Ave., 17th Floor, Chicago., IL 60611-9361. (312) 440-2660   Professional association of dentists who specialize in caring for older people. Sponsors continuing education programs in geriatric dentistry; acts as advocate for increased dental benefits and promotes access to care for older Americans; publishes bimonthly professional journal.

Center for Social Gerontology, 2307 Shelby Ave., Ann Arbor, MI 48103. (313) 665-1126   FAX: (313) 665-2071   Professional organization focused on research, education, technical assistance, and training. Sponsors demonstration projects, conferences, and research (primary concerns— legal rights, employment, guardianship). Provides training programs, technical assistance; publishes training materials, curriculum, quarterly newsletter.

Center for the Study of Aging, 706 Madison Ave., Albany, NY 12208. (518) 462-8105   FAX: (518) 462-1331   National nonprofit resource center that promotes research and training in aging. Provides resource materials (for a fee), technical assistance to researchers, consultation for professionals developing community programs; sponsors conferences and training seminars; maintains a library and provides resource materials; publishes annotated bibliography. Publications available on request.

Episcopal Society for Ministry on Aging, 323 Wyandotte St., Bethlehem, PA 18015. (215) 868-5400   FAX: (215) 691-1682   Nonprofit membership organization of the Episcopal church. Goal is to develop, strengthen, and enable leadership at all levels of the church. Provides religious-oriented materials to members of Episcopal Church; provides educational materials and sponsors networking among church communities and clergy; acts as an advocate and national resource on aging.

The Gerontological Society of America, 1275 K St., NW, Suite 350, Washington, DC 20005-4006. (202) 842-1275   Professional society. Sponsors annual interdisciplinary research meetings encompassing four areas: biological sciences; clinical medicine; psychological and social sciences and social research; planning and practice.

National Academy of Elder Law Attorneys, 655 N. Alvernon Way, Suite 108, Tucson, AZ 85711. (602) 881-4005   FAX: (602) 325-7925   Sponsors educational forums for attorneys specializing in elder law. *Not* a consumer referral service.

National Aging Resource Center on Elder Abuse, College of Human Resources, University of Delaware, Newark, DE 19716. (302) 831-3525   Maintains computer database of all abstracts pertaining to elder abuse; can provide abstracts and articles to consumers. Provides research and technical assistance to police programs and other community programs focusing on elder abuse.

National Association for Home Care, 519 C St., NE, Washington, DC 20002. (202) 547-7424   FAX: (202) 547-3540   Nonprofit trade association. Lobbies on behalf of home care benefits and for home care agencies; offers memberships to businesses that provide these services.

National Association for Senior Living Industries, 184 Duke of Gloucester St; Annapolis, MD 21401-2523. (301) 858-5001   Nonprofit organization of companies and organizations that provide services to the elderly. Sponsors applied research; provides counseling, training, educational programs, and publications to the industry and the general public.

National Council on the Aging (NCOA), 409 3rd St., SW, Suite 200, Washington, DC 20024. (202) 479-1200, 424-9046   FAX: (202) 479-0735   Nonprofit membership organization for professionals who provide services to seniors. Publishes newsletters and journals. Membership includes affiliation with one of the specialty groups housed under the umbrella of NCOA: National Institute of Adult Day Care; National Association of Older Worker Employment Services; National Center on Rural Aging; National Institute on Community-Based Long-Term Care; National Institute of Senior Centers; National Institute of Senior Housing; Health Promotion Institute; National Interfaith Coalition on Aging; National Institute on Financial Issues and Services for Elders; National Voluntary Organization for Independent Living for the Aging; National

Center for Voluntary Leadership in Aging; Family Caregivers of the Aging.

National Institute on Adult Day Care, National Council on the Aging (NCOA) 409 3rd St., SW, Suite 200, Washington, DC 20024. (202) 479-1200, 424-9046   FAX: (202) 479-0735   Private, nonprofit membership organization for professionals. Publishes the *National Voluntary Guidelines for Adult Day Care*. Provides information on care and research; sponsors annual conference. Members receive mailings, journal, newsletter, updates on research grants.

ORGANIZATIONS FOR PROFESSIONALS
AND CONSUMERS

Administration on Aging (AOA), 330 Independence Ave., SW, Washington, DC 20201. (202) 619-0641   Advocacy agency of the U.S. Department of Health and Human Services. Develops programs and coordinates community services for older people. Administers state and area agencies. A range of programs and services are available through these agencies. Refer to local telephone directory or call or write the AOA.

Alzheimer's Disease Education and Referral (ADEAR), National Institute on Aging, # NIAC P. O. Box 8250, Silver Spring, MD 20907. Write to receive free information on Alzheimer's and related disorders.

American Geriatrics Society, 770 Lexington Ave., Suite 300, New York, NY 10021. (212) 308-1414   FAX: (212) 832-8646   Professional organization of physicians and health care providers who specialize in geriatric medicine and health care. Promotes study of geriatrics, provides continuing-education programs, funds research, and accredits training programs. Publishes monthly journal.

American Parkinson's Disease Association, 60 Bam St., Suite 401, Staten Island, New York, NY 10301 (718) 981-8001   HOTLINE INFORMATION: (800) 223-2732 Voluntary organization that funds research and educates public. Patient education materials available. Hotline provides information and referrals to local chapters for services related to Parkinson's disease.

Asociacon Nacional Pro Personas Mayores, (National Association for Hispanic Elderly), National Executive Offices, 3325 Wilshire Blvd., Suite 800, Los Angeles, CA 90010. (213) 487-1922 FAX: (213) 385-3014 Private nonprofit corporation that promotes coalitions nationwide to improve well-being of older Hispanics and other low-income elderly. Administers a nationwide employment program for low-income older persons; provides training and technical assistance to community groups and professionals. Media center publishes and disseminates bilingual information for and about older Hispanics. Provides training and technical assistance to community groups and professionals. National Hispanic Research Center conducts research.

Beverly Foundation, 70 S. Lake Ave., Suite 750; Pasadena, CA 91101. (818) 792-2292 Contact person: Carroll Wendland, Ph.D., President. Primarily a professional organization, with the goal of improving systems and methods of care through research and program development. Also provides caregivers with information about choosing and utilizing nursing homes, retirement communities, home health care, and adult day care. Publishes booklets and educational materials.

Brookdale Center on Aging, 425 E. 25th St., New York, NY 10010-2590. (212) 481-4426 Academic gerontology center founded by Hunter College. Provides professional training and advice to professionals; provides information about research to policy makers and practitioners; sponsors seminars about legal rights of older people. Provides technical assistance to communities; represents clients; respite programs for caregivers of Alzheimer's patients.

Commission on Legal Problems of the Elderly, 1800 M St., NW, Washington, DC 20036. (202) 331-2297 Works to improve the quality of legal services for older citizens; refers clients to appropriate agencies and groups.

Elvirita Lewis Foundation, P. O. Box 1539, LaQuinta, CA 92253. (619) 564-1780 Charitable organization concerned with elder productivity (job placement) and intergenerational programs (child care centers, foster grandparent programs, senior companions). Can provide literature and consultation about instituting and developing programs.

Foundation for Hospice and Home Care, 519 C St., NE, Washington, DC 20002. (202) 547-6586 FAX: (202) 546-8968 Foundation consisting of professional and consumer agencies that provide homemaker and home health services. Provides technical support and guidance to communities that are organizing services; conducts conferences and workshops. Promotes standards of care; administers an accreditation program for service providers. Provides assistance to individuals who are seeking these services in their local area. Publishes newsletter and other materials. (*Family Caregivers' Guide* and *Consumers' Guide to Hospice* are available free; send a stamped, self-addressed envelope.)

Institute on Law and Rights of Older Adults, c/o Brookdale Center on Aging, 425 E. 25th St., New York, NY 10010-2590. (212) 481-4426 Acts as advocate for the legal rights of older people. Conducts seminars for lawyers. Does not deal directly with elderly, but with social workers and lawyers who represent them.

Legal Services for the Elderly, 130 W. 42nd St., 17th Floor, New York, NY 10036-7803. (212) 391-0120 FAX: (212) 719-1939 Advisory center for attorneys who specialize in legal services and issues of older persons. Publications are available on request to general public. Elderly persons can receive referrals to attorneys in their local area.

National Association of Area Agencies on Aging, 1112 16th St., NW, Suite 100, Washington, DC 20036. (202) 296-8130 Represents area agencies on aging nationwide. Acts as an advocate for older persons and agencies; provides addresses of area agencies (also listed in the telephone directory) that provide a variety of services for older Americans; publishes bimonthly newsletter.

National Caucus and Center on Black Aged, 1424 K St., NW, Suite 500, Washington, DC 20005. (202) 637-8400 FAX: (202) 347-0895 Nonprofit organization. Conducts research on black elderly; is creating a national social services network. Sponsors an employment and job-training program; is involved in provision and development of housing services and development for black elderly; coordinates transportation services. Sponsors education and training of professionals; sponsors volunteer programs that encourage community organizations and community advocacy. Publishes newsletter.

National Committee to Preserve Social Security and Medicare, 2000 K St., NW, Suite 800, Washington, DC 20006. (202) 822-9459 HOTLINE ("Senior Flash"): (800) 998-0180 Nonprofit lobby group working on

Social Security and Medicare issues that affect senior citizens. Hotline provides current information about important relevant legislation.

National Council of Senior Citizens, 1331 F St., NW, Washington, DC 20004-1171. (202) 347-8800   FAX: (202) 624-9595   Nonprofit membership organization of clubs, councils, and community groups. Works as advocate for older Americans; distributes information about legislation, Federal programs, benefits, employment, and housing programs. Membership benefits include "Medicare-supplement" health insurance, reduced prices on prescriptions, discount travel. Publishes monthly newsletter.

National Hispanic Council on Aging, 2713 Ontario Rd., NW, Washington, DC 20009. (202) 265-1288   FAX: (202) 745-2522   Private nonprofit organization representing the interests of older Hispanics to government and private sector. Develops and publishes educational materials that are written in Spanish and are geared to specific Hispanic populations. Conducts training institutes, workshops, and conferences for people working with older Hispanics. Publishes free quarterly newsletter and other publications to members.

National Hospice Organization, 1901 N. Moore St., Suite 901, Arlington, VA 22209. (703) 243-5900 (business office)   HELP-LINE: (800) 658-8898 (hospice referral and general information)   Offers memberships to professionals and volunteers. Provides technical advice and training to local hospices; publishes annual directory (*Guide to the National Hospices*). Provides information to individuals about local hospice services.

National Indian Council on Aging, 6400 Uptown Blvd., NE, City Centre, Suite 510-W, Albuquerque, NM 87110. (505) 888-3302   Nonprofit organization concerned with the issues of older Indian and Alaskan Native Americans. Works with agencies serving the older Indian populations; provides training and technical assistance to staffs of tribal organizations; disseminates information; publishes newsletter.

National Institute on Aging (NIA), Information Center, P. O. Box 8057, Gaithersburg, MD 20898-8057. (800) 222-2225   Provides a variety of free informational publications for older people, professionals, and caregivers.

National Institute on Aging (NIA), (Under the National Institutes of Health), Public Information Office, Building 31, Room 5C27, 9000 Rockville Pike, Bethesda, MD 20892. (301) 496-1752   Principal government agency for conducting and supporting research related to the aging process. Prepares and distributes information about issues of interest to older people. Call or write for a listing of specialty topics and research related to the aging process.

National Interfaith Coalition on Aging, c/o National Council on the Aging, 409 Third St., SW, Suite 200, Washington, DC 20024. (202) 479-1200   (800) 424-9046   FAX: (202) 479-0735   Supports research on aging; provides technical assistance and advice to religious groups that serve older people. Provides continuing education to religious leaders and organizations. Maintains a library; produces a quarterly publication.

National Asian Pacific Center on Aging, Melbourne Tower, Suite 914, 1511 3rd Ave., Seattle, WA 98101. (206) 624-1221   FAX: (206) 624-1023   National nonprofit advocacy organization working to improve social service delivery to older Pacific/Asian groups. Provides workshops and technical assistance and training programs to professionals and community groups; can provide information about family and community support groups and services. Publishes a newsletter, service directory, and other publications.

National Senior Citizens Law Center, 1815 H St., NW, Suite 700, Washington, DC 20006. (202) 887-5280   FAX: (202) 785-6792   Public interest law firm specializing in legal problems of the elderly; serves Legal Aid offices and lawyers who offer legal assistance to low-income older people; provides consultation, referrals, information, and publications.

CONSUMER ORGANIZATIONS

Alzheimer's Association, 919 N. Michigan Ave., Suite 1000, Chicago, IL 60611-1676. (800) 272-3900   Provides information on Alzheimer's, as well as referrals to over 220 local chapters that provide information, referrals, support groups, and services in 50 states.

American Association of Retired Persons (AARP), 601 E St., NW, Washington, DC 20049. (202) 434-2277   Consumer membership organization. Local chapters (listed in telephone directory) sponsor educational programs (e.g., crime prevention, consumer protection, income tax preparation). Provides health insurance and investment plans, travel programs. *Women's Initiative Program* provides information about women's needs. *Worker Equity Program* acts as advocate for rights of older workers. *Minority Affairs Program* focuses public attention to needs of minority group elders.

American Health Care Association, 1201 L St., NW, Washington, DC 20005. (202) 842-4444   Provides information and assistance in response to written inquiries; publishes several informative brochures explaining long-term care regulations and what to look for in a good nursing home.

American Red Cross, 430 17th St., NW, Washington, DC 20006. (202) 737-8300   Local chapters provide services to older people free of charge and also provide varied volunteer opportunities for older people.

American Psychiatric Association, National Office, 1400 K St., NW, Washington, DC 20005. (202) 682-6000   Call or write for referrals to a geriatric psychiatrist.

Catholic Golden Age, 430 Penn Ave., Scranton, PA 18505. (717) 342-3294 Nonprofit Catholic membership organization. Provides spiritual benefits as well as discounts on insurance, health care, travel, and so on; publishes quarterly publication. Local chapters plan activities for members.

Children of Aging Parents, Woodbourne Office Campus, 1609 Woodbourne Rd., Suite 302A, Levittown, PA 19057. (215) 945-6900   Nonprofit self-help organization that provides information and support to caregivers of older persons. Provides information and referral service to local services and resources; produces and distributes literature for caregivers. Send stamped, self-addressed envelope (and $1.00 donation) for information.

Choice in Dying, 200 Varick St., New York, NY 10014. (212) 366-5540   Patients' rights organization. Provides state-specific information and health care documents such as living wills, health care proxies, and durable powers of attorney. Provides other information and publications related to end of life decision-making. Provides advice and counsel to families inovlved in the decision-making process.

Elder Craftsmen, 135 E. 65th St., New York, NY 10021. (212) 861-5260   Voluntary nonprofit organization that advises older people in the making and selling of handcrafts. Provides instruction in crafts and marketing; manages retail shop where crafts are sold on consignment. Publishes newsletter and other literature.

Elderhostel, 75 Federal St., Boston, MA 02110. (617) 426-8056 Nonprofit organization that sponsors educational programs for people 60 years old and over. Seminars are conducted nationwide and overseas at universities and colleges; a wide range of low-cost, short-term courses are taught at an introductory level. A catalog of classes is available on request.

Family Services America, 11700 W. Lake Park Dr., Milwaukee, WI 53224. (800) 221-2681 Provides referrals to local agencies that provide programs such as homemaker services to people over 65; provides confidential casework counseling.

Foundation for Hospice and Home Care, 519 C St., NE, Washington, DC 20002. (202) 547-6586 FAX: (202) 546-8968 Consumer organization that provides basic information about home care, services, and patients' rights, as well as information about hospice care and how to go about accessing these services. Publishes newsletter and other publications.

Grandparents' Rights Organization, 555 S. Woodward, Suite 600, Birmingham, MI 48009. (313) 646-7191 National nonprofit organization whose primary goal is to educate grandparents about their rights. Provides information to grandparent members regarding laws, local contact persons, grandparent visitation, custody, and attorneys; supplies support group information for groups in local areas.

Gray Panthers, 2025 Pennsylvania Ave., NW, Suite 821, Washington, DC 20006. (202) 466-3132 FAX: (202) 466-3131 Advocacy group working to eliminate ageism (discrimination based on age). Collects and distributes information, publishes newsletter, provides an information and referral service. Local chapters organize groups to work for better services for older people and sponsor public education seminars.

National Alliance of Senior Citizens, 1700 18th St., NW, Suite 401, Washington, DC 20009. (202) 986-0117 FAX: (202) 986-2974 Policy-oriented membership group for consumers. Acts as advocate and lobbies for policies and programs for older persons. Members receive discounts on health care, phone service, and travel.

National Center for Women and Retirement Research, Long Island University, Southampton, NY 11968. (800) 426-7386 (for information, resources) National organization that conducts seminars and publishes material about financial planning for women of all ages and all walks of life (e.g., a guidebook: "Looking Ahead to Your Financial Future"; a videotape: "Women and Money: Things Your Mother Never Told You About Finances"). Provides resources nationwide; is establishing regional offices.

National Citizens' Coalition for Nursing Home Reform, 1224 M St., NW, Suite 301, Washington, DC 20005. (202) 393-2018 FAX: (202) 393-4122 Composed of 300 nationwide citizen advocacy groups; directed towards empowerment of consumers and advocates. National information clearinghouse. Provides legislative advocacy as well as assistance in resolving individual complaints and problems; supports resident and family councils and other forms of consumer empowerment.

Nursing Home Information Service, National Council of Senior Citizens, National Senior Citizens Education and Research Center, 1331 F St., NW, Washington, DC 20004-1171. (202) 347-8800 Referral center for consumers of long-term care services. Offers information on nursing homes and alternative community and health services, as well as information on how to select a nursing home.

Older American Volunteer Programs, c/o ACTION, 1100 Vermont Ave., NW, Washington, DC 20525. (202) 606-4855 Federal government agency that sponsors volunteer programs conducted by older adults: *Foster Grandparents Program* for children with special needs (volunteers care for physically, emotionally, or mentally disabled children in institutions and private settings); *Retired Senior Volunteer Program* (RSVP) (volunteers work in schools, courts, libraries, day-care centers, hospitals, community service centers); *Senior Companion Program* (volunteers help other older persons remain in their own homes or provide extra support when they have special health, education, and social needs).

Older Women's League, 666 11th St., NW, Suite 700, Washington, DC 20001. (202) 783-6686 FAX: (202) 638-2356 Works as advocate for concerns of older women through public policy reform and provision of mutual aid and supportive services (through local chapters). Operates speakers' bureau and distributes educational materials; publishes monthly newsletter.

National Shut-In Society, 1925 N. Lynn St., Suite 500, Rosslyn, VA 22209

(703) 516-6770   Private nonprofit organization whose members provide written and telephone correspondence as well as visitation to home-bound persons. Publishes bimonthly magazine. Call for number of local chapter to volunteer or to receive services.

Senior Action in a Gay Environment, Inc. (SAGE), Serving the Older Gay Community, 208 W. 13th St., New York, NY 10011. (212) 741-2247   Membership organization working with the support of the United Way. Acts as advocate for policy issues related to gay and lesbian older Americans; provides technical assistance and guidance for local groups dedicated to the gay senior community. Conducts pen pal program; has publications for members.

United Seniors Health Cooperative, 1331 H St., NW, Suite 500, Washington, DC 20005-4706. (202) 393-6222   Private nonprofit organization for members. Offers discounts on home care and health care; provides insurance information; publishes bimonthly newsletters. A list of materials is available on request.

Widowed Person's Service, AARP, 601 E St., NW, Washington, DC 20049. (202) 434-2277   Outreach program for newly widowed persons. Provides group sessions, publications about legal matters, volunteer opportunities, and other services.

AUTHOR INDEX

SUBJECT INDEX